Adventures in the Deeps of the Mind

Princeton Essays in Literature
Advisory Committee: Joseph Bauke, Robert Fagles,
Claudio Guillen, Robert Maguire
For a listing of all titles, see page 151

Adventures in the Deeps of the Mind

The Cuchulain Cycle of W. B. Yeats

Barton R. Friedman

Princeton University Press

Princeton, New Jersey

Copyright © 1977 by Princeton University Press
Published by Princeton University Press,
Princeton, New Jersey
In the United Kingdom: Princeton University Press,
Guildford, Surrey

Library of Congress Cataloging in Publication Data will
be found on the last printed page of this book

Publication of this book has been aided by a grant
from the Lacy Lockert Fund

This book has been composed in VIP Aldus

Printed in the United States of America
by Princeton University Press, Princeton, New Jersey

To
my mother and father
and to
Sheila
who danced Emer in *The Death of Cuchulain*

Contents

Acknowledgments

I wish to thank the editors of the *Arizona Quarterly* and the *Journal of Modern Literature* for permission to reprint sections of this book originally appearing in their pages. I wish also to thank the Graduate School of the University of Wisconsin-Madison for a grant which freed me during the summer of 1974 to write my first draft.

During that summer I had the very able help of Ms. Kenith Simmons, who read and criticized each chapter as I wrote it, and throughout of my wife, Sheila, to whom this book is partly dedicated. I owe a special debt too to my friend and one-time teaching colleague in English 478 ("Shaw and Anglo-Irish Drama") at the University of Wisconsin, John J. Pirri, whose many conversations with me on Yeats's plays may have influenced this book more than either of us knows, and to those students in the course who, valuing the educational process above mere grades, had the courage to say, "I don't think so."

Quotations from the works of W.B. Yeats are reprinted with permission of M.B. Yeats, Miss Anne Yeats and the Macmillan Co. of London and Basingstoke, and of Macmillan Publishing Co., Inc. of New York as follows:

"Adam's Curse"—Copyright 1903 by Macmillan Publishing Co., Inc. Renewed 1931 by William Butler Yeats. "The Wanderings of Oisin"—Copyright 1906 by Macmillan Publishing Co., Inc. Renewed 1934 by William Butler Yeats. "September 1913," "To a Shade," and "The Two Kings"—Copyright 1916 by Macmillan Publishing Co., Inc. Renewed 1944 by Bertha Georgie Yeats. "Ego Dominus Tuus"—Copyright 1918 by Macmillan Publishing Co., Inc. Renewed 1946 by Bertha Georgie Yeats. "Among School Children" and "Sailing to Byzantium"—Copyright 1928 by Macmillan Publishing Co., Inc. Renewed 1956 by Bertha Georgie Yeats. "Byzantium"—Copyright 1933 by Macmillan Publishing Co., Inc. Renewed 1961 by Bertha Georgie Yeats. "The Circus Animals' Desertion," "Cuchulain Comforted," "Lapis Lazuli" and "The

Introduction

Once, some years ago, I asked a dancer at Mills College why nobody performed Yeats's plays. "Nobody," she replied, "understands them"—meaning in part that she could imagine no way in which they might be effectively staged. This skepticism about their stageability persists, even among literary critics who otherwise account themselves admirers of Yeats. In *Yeats's VISION and the Later Plays* (1963), one of the first serious studies of his drama, Helen Vendler had pronounced the plays "dramatic neither in conception nor in end," arguing that they are rather vehicles for lyrics.[1] And in an article as current as September, 1974 Kathleen M. Vogt, evincing a comparable uneasiness specifically about *At the Hawk's Well*, adjudges that earliest of Yeats's plays for dancers enigmatic and unfinished.[2]

Such reactions, from thoughtful and sympathetic witnesses, would surely have frustrated the playwright who had insisted, a decade before *At the Hawk's Well*, that he viewed "the play written to be read only as . . . imperfect," adding that the "writer of drama must observe the form as carefully as if it were a sonnet. . . ."[3] Yet even Reg Skene, whose recent book, *The Cuchulain Plays of W.B. Yeats*, presumably emerged, at least to some degree, from his direction of the cycle at the University of Winnipeg, contributes little to our meager store of ideas about how, or whether, this drama works dramatically. Though Skene explores at painstaking length the ritualistic dimension of the plays, schematizing them by the lunar wheel in *A Vision* and the cycle of the seasons, he displays to me no real awareness that a ritual succeeds alone by inducing a communion between actors and audience. The impression of the Cuchul-

[1] *Yeat's VISION and the Later Plays* (Cambridge, Mass.: Harvard University Press, 1963), p. 141.

[2] "Counter-Components in Yeats's *At the Hawk's Well*," *Modern Drama*, xvii (1974), 319.

[3] From *The Poetical Works of William B. Yeats*, vol. ii, *Dramatic Poems* (1907). See *The Variorum Edition of the Plays of W.B. Yeats*, ed. Russell K. Alspach (New York: Macmillan, 1969), pp. 1293–94.

ain plays unfolding from his pages relates at best tenuously to
the experience of the spectator in the theater.

 , Their composition extending almost throughout Yeats's
career, from the beginning of *On Baile's Strand* in 1901 to *The
Death of Cuchulain* in 1939, these plays (and I include *Deirdre*
as well as those centering on Cuchulain himself) nonetheless
encompass a paradigm of Yeats's struggle—I would claim his
triumphant struggle—to find a genuinely dramatic mode
adequate to his aspirations for the stage. That they (despite
F.A.C. Wilson's assertion to the contrary) in fact comprise a cycle, and not a random series of pieces joined merely by dependence on a common source, Skene emphasizes, citing Yeats's
note to *On Baile's Strand*, from *Poems, 1899–1905* (1906), that
"It is one of a cycle of plays dealing with Cuchulain, with his
friends and enemies. One of these plays will have Aoife as its
central character, and the principal motive of another will be the
power of the witches over Cuchulain's life."[4] In this statement,
written with only the first of the Cuchulain plays behind him
and *Deirdre* no more than underway, Yeats adumbrates virtually the whole sequence.

Skene roots Yeats's plan to build a cycle around the hero of
the *Táin Bó Cailnge* in his revision of *On Baile's Strand*;[5]
whereas Yeats's own testimony suggests that he began thinking
and working toward this goal much earlier. Writing to (as he
believed) Fiona MacLeod in January, 1897, he had announced
that, "After these books [*The Shadowy Waters* and an un-
named novel, perhaps *John Sherman*] I start a long-cherished
project—a poetical version of the great Celtic epic tale, Deirdre,
Cuchullin at the Ford, and Cuchullin's death, and Dermot and
Grainne." And he was to reiterate his commitment to this
scheme with every step toward its realization. Cheered by a
successful revival of *On Baile's Strand*, he wrote to John Quinn

[4] *The Cuchulain Plays of W.B.Yeats* (London: Macmillan, 1974), p. ix. For
the passage in context, see *The Variorum Plays*, p. 526. For Wilson's view that
Four Plays for Dancers, not the Cuchulain dramas, comprise Yeats's one attempt at a dramatic cycle, see *Yeats's Iconography* (London: Victor Gollancz,
1960), p. 4.

[5] *The Cuchulain Plays of W.B. Yeats*, p. 48.

in June, 1915—as he was gestating *At the Hawk's Well*—that "All my mythological people have come alive again and I want to complete my heroic cycle." Reflecting some ten months later, in "Certain Noble Plays of Japan," on the production he had staged in Lady Cunard's drawing room, he was to observe that, "When this play and its performance run as smoothly as my skill can make them, I shall hope to write another of the same sort and so complete a dramatic celebration of the life of Cuchulain planned long ago." Introducing the prose version of that other play in *Wheels and Butterflies* (1934), he recalls that "I wrote in blank verse, which tried to bring as close to common speech as the subject permitted, a number of connected plays—*Deirdre, At the Hawk's Well, The Green Helmet, On Baile's Strand, The Only Jealousy of Emer.* I would have attempted the Battle of the Ford and the Death of Cuchulain, had not the mood of Ireland changed."[6]

The connectedness of these plays lies not alone in the evolution of their hero from the untried youth seeking the Well of Immortality in *At the Hawk's Well* to the doomed giant remaking his mythic self in *The Death of Cuchulain* but in the evolution of their playwright from the imitator of Shakespeare in the first version of *On Baile's Strand* to the finisher of the myth of his innermost self, again in *The Death of Cuchulain.* The cycle, that is, traces the playwright's progress toward psychodrama. In his voluminous study of Yeats's work Harold Bloom argues that Yeats deduced from his reading in *Noh* the solution to a problem vexing his Romantic precursors: how to devise a form suited to "their intricate sensibilities."[7] While Bloom's phrase seems to me vague, it hints at one of Yeats's real accomplishments. The efforts of the Romantic poets to write plays had repeatedly come a cropper of their failure to find ways of staging the deeps of the mind. Yeats found a way.

[6] For the letters to Fiona MacLeod and John Quinn, see *The Letters of W.B. Yeats*, ed. Allan Wade (New York: Macmillan, 1955), pp. 280 and 595 respectively. For the observation from "Certain Noble Plays," see *Essays and Introductions* (New York: Macmillan, 1961), pp. 221–22. For the comment on *Fighting the Waves*, see *The Variorum Plays*, pp. 567–68.

[7] *Yeats* (New York: Oxford University Press, 1970), p. 293.

Adventures in the Deeps of the Mind

I

Toward Staging the Deeps of the Mind

On August 11, 1901, Yeats wrote to T. Sturge Moore: "I am starting a little heroical play about Cuchullin and am curious to see how my recent practical experience of the stage will affect my work."[1] By "recent practical experience of the stage," Yeats doubtless meant his struggles on behalf of the budding Irish dramatic movement and his part in the production of his own two earlier plays, *The Land of Heart's Desire* in 1894 and *The Countess Cathleen* in 1899. But he may also have meant his visit to Stratford-on-Avon of April, 1901, during which he had seen most of the Henriad, and about which he had written eloquently and enthusiastically in *The Speaker* that May:

> The five plays, that are but one play [emended to "six plays, that are but one play" in *Ideas of Good and Evil*] have, when played one after another, something extravagant and superhuman, something almost mythological. Those nobles with their indifference to death and their immense energy seem at times no nearer the common stature of men than do the Gods and the heroes of Greek plays. Had there been no Renaissance and no Italian influence to bring in the stories of other lands English history would, it may be, have become as important to the English imagination as the Greek Myths to the Greek imagination; and many plays by many poets would have woven it into a single story whose contours, vast as those of Greek myth, would have made living men and women seem like swallows building their nests under the architrave of some Temple of the Giants. English literature, because it would have grown out of itself, might have had the simplicity and unity of Greek literature, for I can never get out of my head that no man, even though he be Shakespeare, can write perfectly when his web is woven of threads that have been spun in many lands.[2]

[1] *W.B.Yeats and T. Sturge Moore Their Correspondence*, ed. Ursula Bridge (London: Routledge & Kegan Paul, 1953), p. 2.

[2] For the date of Yeats's first visit to Stratford, see Rupin W. Desai, *Yeats's Shakespeare* (Evanston, Illinois: Northwestern University Press, 1971), p. 8.

3

That *On Baile's Strand*, Yeats's "little heroical play about Cuchullin," shows the imprint of the Henriad is manifest not alone from its double-plot—where the Blind Man and Fool anticipate by parody Cuchulain's oath-taking, as the prince and Falstaff anticipate Hal's confrontation with his Father in *1 Henry IV*—but from what Yeats had at first intended as Conchubar's opening speech, which parallels Henry's opening speech to his court. Henry begins, wishing for the return of peace to his realm:

> So shaken as we are, so wan with care,
> Find we a time for frighted peace to pant,
> And breathe short-winded accents of new broils
> To be commenced in stronds afar remote.

(I.i.1–4)

Conchubar begins, hailing the return of peace to his realm:

> I have called you hither Kings of Ullad, and Kings
> Of Muirthemne and Conal Muirthemne,
> And tributary Kings, for now there is peace—

(262–64)[3]

Henry proposes a penitential crusade partly to confirm the order of rank and privilege, upon which his kingdom depends:

> those opposed eyes,
> Which, like the meteors of a troubled heaven,
> All of one nature, of one substance bred,
> Did lately meet in the intestine shock
> And furious close of civil butchery,
> Shall now, in mutual well-beseeming ranks,
> March all one way and be no more opposed
> Against acquaintance, kindred and allies.

(9–16)

Yeats's famous essay on Shakespeare, "At Stratford-on-Avon," appeared in two installments in *The Speaker* for 11 and 18 May, 1901. The passage quoted occurs in the number for 18 May, p. 158.

[3] Quotations of earlier, subsequently altered or deleted passages of *On Baile's Strand*, as well as other plays discussed in this study, are from *The Variorum Plays*. For this speech, see pp. 490–92.

Conchubar proposes the restoration of Emain Macha to the same end:

> It's time to build up Emain that was burned
> At the outsetting of these wars; for we
> being the foremost men, should have high chairs
> And be much stared at and wondered at, and speak
> Out of more laughing overflowing hearts
> Than common men.
>
> (265–70)

Henry concedes that his designs continue to be thwarted by civil strife:

> But this our purpose now is twelve months old,
> And bootless tis to tell you we will go.
> Therefore we meet not now: . . .
>
> (29–31)

Conchubar acknowledges that his designs have, at least in the past, been thwarted by like eruptions:

> . . . many a time
> I would have called you hither to this work
> But always, when I'd all but summoned you,
> Some war or some rebellion would break out.
>
> (274–77)

Yeats's attempt at blank verse in Conchubar's address pales beside Shakespeare's (or beside his own in the 1906 reworking of *On Baile's Strand*, as well as in later plays), which sufficiently explains its deletion. In deleting it, however, he fundamentally changed the conflict in the play, replacing Conchubar's desire to rebuild Emain with his demand that Cuchulain take an oath.

The introduction of the oath gives the play, as Skene properly observes, an organic unity lacking in the original version.[4] It also sharpens the parallel between *On Baile's Strand* and the Henriad, crystallizing the issue of fealty to the throne as a major thematic focus. Yeats, though, redefines the issue to suit his own moral design, turning the play into a clash between

[4] *The Cuchulain Plays of W.B. Yeats*, p. 157.

reason, measure, bourgeois pragmatism and imagination, freedom, Blakean excess.[5] In so doing he believes himself to be reasserting true Shakespearean values against the distortions of (mainly Edward Dowden's) smug Victorian empiricism. As he argues in his essay on Shakespeare:

> The deeds of Coriolanus, Hamlet, Timon, Richard II. had no obvious use, were, indeed, no more than the expression of their personalities, and so it was thought Shakespeare was accusing them, and telling us to be careful lest we deserve the like accusations. It did not occur to the critics that you cannot know a man from his actions, because you cannot watch him in every kind of circumstance, and that men are made useless to the State as often by abundance as by emptiness, and that a man's business may at times be revelation, and not reformation. Fortinbras, was, it is likely enough, a better King than Hamlet would have been, Aufidius was a more reasonable man than Coriolanus, Henry V. was a better man-at-arms than Richard II., but, after all, were not those others who changed nothing for the better and many things for the worse greater in the Divine Hierarchies?[6]

Rupin W. Desai argues in his book, *Yeats's Shakespeare*, that Yeats found in the history plays a spectrum of the modes of political conduct exhibited by man, and that he read into the defeat of Richard by the ruthless empiricist, Henry, an allegory of Ireland's oppression by England.[7] What Yeats seems primarily to be suggesting in "At Stratford-on-Avon," however, is that Shakespeare—even in his history plays—was only incidentally concerned with history; that, like Yeats himself, he was creating a personal myth, depicting the alienation suffered by the ar-

---

[5] Thomas Parkinson defines this conflict analogously in *W.B.Yeats, Self-Critic* (Berkeley: The University of California Press, 1951), p. 54, arguing that the major conflict of Yeats's Abbey plays in general—his examples are *On Baile's Strand* and *The King's Threshold*—lies in the struggle between a "fixed palpable world of human affairs" and a "world of passion and aspiration . . . beyond reason, system, or office."

[6] "At Stratford-on-Avon," *The Speaker* (May 18, 1901), 185.

[7] See especially pp. 16 and 20.

tistic personality. Richard II abused by nineteenth-century critics of Shakespeare, is, for Yeats, akin to the frail, bespectacled student persecuted for his Irishness and his father's vocation, whom he portrays as his younger self in *Reveries over Childhood and Youth*. Both are victims of bourgeois vulgarity. The boys at Hammersmith gathering around him to ask, "Who's your father?" "What does he do?" "How much money has he?" weigh equally on Yeats's moral scale with the authors of those books he found in the library at Stratford, who "took the same delight in abasing Richard II that schoolboys do in persecuting some boy of fine temperament, who has weak muscles and a distaste for school games."[8]

While Shakespeare, as Yeats read him, was kept from a perfect realization of his myth by the burden his cultural heritage laid upon him—that Renaissance and Italian influence bringing in the stories of other lands—Yeats saw himself, in fact all the Abbey dramatists, bearing no such burden. As resuscitators of a tradition almost moribund, they were inheriting a subject uncontaminated by foreign matter. When Lady Gregory in 1902 published her redaction of the *Táin Bó Cailnge, Cuchulain of Muirthemne*, Yeats proclaimed it "the best book that has ever come out of Ireland," exulting that "If we will but tell these stories to our children the Land will begin again to be a Holy Land as it was before men gave their hearts to Greece and Rome and Judea."[9] Dramatizing the legend behind *On Baile's Strand*, Yeats was embarking on his project for telling these stories, if not to the children of Ireland, then to a public which could transmit them to their children. "The play," he had confided to Moore, "is part of a greater scheme. I am doing all the chief stories of the first heroic age in Ireland in a series of poems."[10] Though he was never to finish this greater scheme, his ambition to do all the chief stories of the first heroic age in Ireland was by

[8] "At Stratford-on-Avon," *The Speaker* (May 18, 1901), 185. For the episode in *Reveries*, see *The Autobiography of William Butler Yeats* (New York: Macmillan, 1965), p. 20.

[9] From his Preface to *Cuchulain of Muirthemne*, reprinted in *Explorations* (London: Macmillan, 1962), pp. 3–13. For the passages quoted, see pp. 3 and 12–13.

[10] *W.B. Yeats and T. Sturge Moore*, p. 2.

the end of his life to yield his own five (or six) plays that are but one play, the Cuchulain cycle.

Yeats's recurrence to Cuchulain as an embodiment of his idealized self—the artist projected into his opposite, the contemplative into the active man—constitutes his major effort to awake from the nightmare of history, to grasp the simplicity and unity of which he felt Shakespeare had been deprived. It was his success in attaining this mythic purity that Yeats most admired about Synge:

> Synge, like all the great kin, sought the race, not through the eyes or in history, or even in the future, but where those monks [of Mont-Saint-Michel] found God, in the depths of the mind, and in all art like his, although it does not command—indeed because it does not—may lie the roots of far-branching events.[11]

Synge appears to Yeats to be engaged in that same quarrel with the world dramatized in *On Baile's Strand* through the conflict of Conchubar and Cuchulain, or in *The King's Threshold* through that of Guaire and Seanchan. His art denies value to material reality, manifest either in an apprehensible present, a documentable past, or a hypothetical future, seeking instead the transcendent truth to be found in imagination. It becomes for Yeats a paradigmatic expression of the ideal to which every artist must aspire: "All art is the disengaging of a soul from place and history, its suspension in a beautiful or terrible light to await the Judgment, though it must be, seeing that all days were a Last Day, judged already."[12]

Yeats dates his eulogy for Synge September 14, 1910. But the phrase he uses to locate the focus of Synge's drama, "in the depths of the mind," anticipates his account six years later of the effect achieved by Michio Ito dancing the Guardian in *At the Hawk's Well*, whom Yeats describes as receding from the audience "to inhabit as it were the deeps of the mind."[13] That Yeats

---

[11] "J.M. Synge and the Ireland of His Time," *Essays and Introductions*, p. 341.

[12] *Ibid.*, p. 339.

[13] "Certain Noble Plays of Japan," p. 224.

understands the deeps of the mind as the part of man's psyche opening into the *Anima Mundi*, and drama as a vehicle for attuning him to this innermost aspect of himself, is suggested, even in the essay on Synge, by his claim that it was there Synge sought the race. The *Anima Mundi* is the consciousness of the race. Seeing in Ito's performance, as he recalls it in "Certain Noble Plays of Japan," "the tragic image that has stirred my imagination," Yeats identifies him with an archetype of that consciousness, an image out of *Anima Mundi* itself.[14]

In *Per Amica Silentia Lunae*, published some thirteen months after the performance of *At the Hawk's Well*, and the essay he wrote commemorating the performance, Yeats hypothesizes that "if all our mental images no less than apparitions (and I see no reason to distinguish) are forms existing in the general vehicle of *Anima Mundi*, and mirrored in our particular vehicle, many crooked things are made straight."[15] His particular vehicle is the artifact—poem or play. For he ascribes to the imagination magical power. Recounting his own quest for the image, again in *Per Amica Silentia Lunae*, he reports having "always sought to bring my mind close to the mind of Indian and Japanese poets, old women in Connaught, mediums in Soho, lay brothers whom I imagine dreaming in some mediaeval monastery the dreams of their village, learned authors who refer all to antiquity"; and he proposes as the reward of his efforts at communion with this diversity of kindred spirits that it enables him to immerse his mind "in the general mind where that mind is scarce separable from what we have begun to call 'the subconscious'. . . ."

Immersing his mind in the general mind frees Yeats from the demands of circumstantial realism, "from all that comes of councils and committees, from the world as it is seen from universities or from populous towns. . . ." He suggests, moreover, that achieving this freedom involves a discipline, consciously cultivated: "I have murmured evocations and frequented mediums, delighted in all that displayed great problems through sensuous images, or exciting phrases, accepting from

[14] The quotation is from "Certain Noble Plays," p. 224.

[15] *Per Amica Silentia Lunae* (London: Macmillan, 1918), p. 63.

abstract schools but a few technical words that are so old they seem but broken architraves fallen amid brambles and grass, and have put myself to school where all things are seen . . ."[16]

Yeats is adducing the evidence of his own creative experience to assert the potential of the imagination to transport the self and transform reality. He had, however, been portraying this potential dramatically at least since *The King's Threshold* (1904), where the Oldest Pupil answers Seanchan's question, "Why poetry is honoured," by proclaiming that "the poets hung/ Images of the life that was in Eden/ About the child-bed of the world, that it,/ Looking upon those images, might bear/ Triumphant children" (125 and 128–32).[17] Or again, as he observes of Synge, in art like his may lie the roots of far-branching events, a perpetual adumbration of the Last Day.

Such statements of the influence exerted by art and the ways in which that influence may be grasped, from *The King's Threshold*, or "J.M. Synge and the Ireland of His Time," or *Per Amica Silentia Lunae*, differ in substance not at all from Yeats's famous profession of belief in magic, written the same year he began *On Baile's Strand*. The magical evocation, like that of art, is said to take place "in the depths of the mind." The reverie drawing the magician, or the artist, into the mind's depths joins his mind and memory to what Yeats calls in his essay the "great mind and great memory." And this reverie—which is to say, the process of art as of magic—expands consciousness.[18]

David R. Clark in his provocative little book, *W.B. Yeats and the Theatre of Desolate Reality*, defines one aspect of the consciousness expanding tendencies to Yeats's art: arguing that while his plays comprehend the whole of what Francis Fergusson terms tragic rhythm, the movement from purpose to passion to perception, most of them dramatize only the step from passion to perception; that they are recognition scenes.[19] Yeats

---

[16] *Ibid.*, pp. 45–46.

[17] Richard Ellmann, *Eminent Domain* (New York: Oxford University Press, 1967), p. 120, argues that *The King's Threshold* "reads like a dramatic demonstration of 'The Symbolism of Poetry' and 'Magic'."

[18] "Magic," *Essays and Introductions*, p. 28.

[19] *W.B. Yeats and the Theatre of Desolate Reality* (Dublin: The Dolmen Press, 1965), p. 16.

was interested, though, not alone in staging recognition scenes but in extending the experience of recognition to the audience, in effecting the communion between artist and audience he had learned, chiefly perhaps from Shelley, to admire about Greek tragedy. In *The Defence of Poetry*, from which Yeats was to quote at length in his important essay, "The Philosophy of Shelley's Poetry," and which he was to make a cornerstone of the metaphysic underlying *The King's Threshold* (published in its first English edition as a companion piece to *On Baile's Strand*), Shelley had observed that "the pleasure resulting from the manner in which [poets] express the influence of society or nature upon their own minds, communicates itself to others, and gathers a sort of reduplication from that community." This reduplication he finds exemplified in those he calls the Athenian poets, through whose work "The imagination is enlarged by a sympathy with pains and passions so mighty that they distend in their conception and capacity of that by which they are conceived. . . ."[20]

Or, as Yeats himself argues in "The Tragic Theatre" (1910), "tragedy must always be a drowning and breaking of the dykes that separate man from man. . . ."[21] The drowning and breaking of the dykes separating man from man is what he dramatizes at the beginning of *At the Hawk's Well*, presenting the audience not with a painted scene but with three Musicians on a bare stage calling "to the eye of the mind" the rudiments of a scene. The Musicians are inviting the audience to participate in the experience of creating the scene, to render for themselves the choked well and stripped boughs of the mountainside where the Old Man waits.

At the Hawk's Well is in this sense—like Yeats's descrip-

[20] For these quotations from *The Defence*, see *The Complete Works of Percy Bysshe Shelley*, vol. VII, ed. Roger Ingpen and Walter Peck (New York: The Gordian Press, 1965), pp. 111 and 121.

[21] *Essays and Introductions*, p. 241. Edward Engelberg in his extremely valuable study of Yeats's aesthetic, *The Vast Design* (Toronto: The University of Toronto Press, 1964), p. 6, also points out the apparent debt of "The Tragic Theatre" to Shelley's discussion of Greek tragedy in *The Defence*. Engelberg quotes in support of his position another passage from Yeats's essay, the rhetoric of which is admittedly closer to Shelley's than the one I have cited, but which seems to me finally less revealing of Yeats's concept of drama.

tive-meditative poems (say "The Wild Swans at Coole" or "Among School Children") or the last chapter in his Cuchulain saga, *The Death of Cuchulain*—about its own composition. Its setting is the mind of the playwright gestating the play, its triumph the attainment of a method for inducing the audience to live that process: to become for the dramatic moment artists shaping an artifact.[22]

That drama is, or should be, pre-eminently a concretizing of psychic, even creative energies Yeats had concluded long before, in part from his study of Blake. "By the imagination," he had written in the commentary to the edition he and Edwin Ellis had published in 1893, "Blake means, among other things, the sympathetic will or love that makes us travel from mental state to mental state and surround ourselves with their personified images, for all imaginative perceptions are personified feelings."[23] Yeats thus seeks to define Blake's understanding of how symbols get made:

> The most perfect truth is simply the dramatic expression of the most complete man. . . . This poetic genius or central mood in all things is that which creates all by affinity— worlds no less than religions or philosophies. First, a bodiless mood, and then a surging thought, and last a thing. This

[22] That the action of *At the Hawk's Well* occurs in the mind has at least nominally been recognized by several critics. Richard Ellmann, *Yeats: the Man and the Masks* (New York: E.P. Dutton, 1948), p. 215, locates the scenario in the mind's eye. Leonard E. Nathan, *The Tragic Drama of William Butler Yeats: Figures in a Dance* (New York: Columbia University Press, 1965), pp. 154–55, suggests that Yeats found in *Noh* a vehicle for making natural reality mirror spiritual reality—what Nathan calls the war of the orders—in the mind's depths. Clark in *W.B. Yeats and the Theatre of Desolate Reality*, p. 20, generalizes about Yeats's dramatic method that, for him, action is significant insofar as it imitates psychic action. John Rees Moore, *Masks of Love and Death: Yeats as Dramatist* (Ithaca: Cornell University Press, 1971), p. 15, observes that after Yeats stopped writing for the Abbey in 1910, he shifted his focus inward. None of these critics, however, adequately traces the internalization of Yeats's dramatic focus, which, it seems to me, is rooted in his very earliest attempts both at drama and at a theory of drama. And none of them sees the relation between this focus and his interest in staging the creative process itself.

[23] *The Poetical Works of William Blake*, vol. i (London: Bernard Quaritch, 1893), p. 276.

triad is universal, and corresponds to Father, Son, and Holy Spirit.[24]

The products of the deepest inspiration are, to use a word both Yeats and Blake would probably have loathed, allegorical, consisting in embodied emanations of the artist's mind: "We perceive the world through countless little reflections of our own image."[25]

Embodying emanations of the artist's mind sums up Yeats's idea of drama from his earliest theoretical pronouncements on the stage. In what is perhaps the most famous of his remarks on dramatic genre, appearing in *Samhain* for 1904, he argues that farce and tragedy function alike, each isolating one action from all other actions, each encapsulating "a moment of intense life"; and that, because the moment the play evokes is a moment set apart, "The characters . . . involved in it are freed from everything . . . not a part of that action . . . it is an energy, an eddy of life purified from everything but itself."[26] Figures in Yeatsian drama are not characters (in what Yeats might have considered the Ibsenite conception of character) but aspects of a character: personified ideas, emotions, impulses insulated from all other ideas, emotions, impulses.

In proposing this decidedly anti-realistic conception of character Yeats again was drawing on his studies of Blake and Shelley. Distinguishing between poem and story in his *Defence*, Shelley defines a poem as "the creation of actions according to the unchangeable forms of human nature, as existing in the mind of the creator, which is itself the image of all other minds."[27] And Blake types Chaucer's pilgrims in his "Descriptive Catalogue" as "a description of the eternal Principles that exist in all ages," identifying the Plowman as "simplicity itself, with wisdom and strength for its stamina," as "Hercules in his supreme eternal state, divested of his spectrous shadow; which is the Miller. . . ."[28] Yeats, indeed, essentially repeats these

[24] *Ibid.*, p. 241.   [25] *Ibid.*, p. 276.

[26] Reprinted in *Explorations*, pp. 153–54.

[27] *Complete Works*, vol. VII, p. 115.

[28] "A Descriptive Catalogue of Pictures, Poetical and Historical Inventions," *The Poetry and Prose of William Blake*, ed. David Erdman, comm. Harold Bloom (Garden City, New York: Doubleday & Company, Inc., 1970), p. 257.

Blakean and Shelleyan views in "The Tragic Theatre," declaring that in tragedy "The persons upon the stage . . . greaten until they are humanity itself."[29]

He is saying in effect that the tragic figure behaves singlemindedly, obsessively. He becomes what he enacts, which is to say, he becomes what Yeats calls a Daimon. The Daimon, to Yeats, is the opposite that the poet poetizing absorbs into himself: "when I shut my door and light the candle," writes Yeats, describing his own experience of the creative process in *Per Amica Silentia Lunae*, "I invite a marmorean Muse, an art where no thought or emotion has come to mind because another man has thought or felt something different, for now there must be no reaction, action only, and the world must move my heart but to the heart's discovery of itself, and I begin to dream of eyelids that do not quiver before the bayonet: all my thoughts have ease and joy, I am all virtue and confidence."[30]

The heart's discovery of itself consists in envisioning a form fearless, immortal, free of the laws inherent in the human condition ("eyelids that do not quiver before the bayonet"). Art, that is, consists in the artist making a myth of himself. Man and Daimon are wed, Yeats asserts, again in *Per Amica Silentia Lunae*, "when the man has found a mask whose lineaments permit the expression of all the man most lacks, and it may be dreads, and of that only."[31] In *At the Hawk's Well* Cuchulain and the Old Man wear masks, while the Musicians and the Guardian have their faces made up to resemble masks. Leonard E. Nathan suggests that Yeats distinguished thereby between primary participants in the action and human observers of the action (the Guardian being human too until possessed by the Woman of the *Sidhe*).[32] But Cuchulain in his temerity and activity also images what the artist, the man of contemplation, most lacks, and the Old Man in his timidity and atrophy what he most dreads.

Neither mask nor musician, however, is a device Yeats intro-

---

[29] *Essays and Introductions*, p. 241.
[30] *Per Amica Silentia Lunae*, p. 10.   [31] *Ibid.*, p. 22.
[32] *The Tragic Drama of W.B. Yeats*, p. 183.

duced into his drama through *At the Hawk's Well*. As early as 1899, he was writing to the editor of the *Daily Chronicle*:

> We have forgotten that the Drama began in the chanted ode, and that whenever it has been great it has been written certainly to delight our eyes, but to delight our ears more than our eyes. Greek actors with masks upon their faces, and their stature increased by artifice, must have been content to delight the eyes with but an austere and monotonous beauty, and Elizabethan actors who had to speak so much that would seem irrelevant poetry to modern audiences must have thought oratory a principal part of acting.[33]

In this claim he was yet again echoing Shelley, who, attacking modern theater in his *Defence*, had complained that, among other things, "We have tragedy without music and dancing . . . [and that] Our system of divesting the actor's face of a mask, on which the many expressions appropriated to his dramatic character might be moulded into one permanent and unchanging expression, is favourable only to a partial and inharmonious effect. . . ."[34] And by 1910, Yeats was already seeking to translate these pronouncements into practice, writing to Lady Gregory on October 21 of his plans to experiment with masks for *The Hour-Glass*, then adding: "If the masks work right I would put the fool and blind man in *Baile's Strand* into masks. . . . I should also like the Abbey to be the first modern theatre to use the mask."[35]

This desire to make the Abbey the first modern theater to use

[33] Wade, *Letters*, p. 309.

[34] *Complete Works*, vol. VII, pp. 119–20.

[35] Wade, *Letters*, p. 554. Citing Yeats's Note on *The Hour-Glass* from *Plays for an Irish Theatre*, Skene suggests (*Cuchulain Plays*, p. 45) that, "under the influence of Gordon Craig," Yeats was considering masks for the Blind Man and Fool of *On Baile's Strand* as early as 1906. But *Plays for an Irish Theatre* appeared in 1911, and the passage Skene points to seems clearly a rephrasing of Yeats's letter to Lady Gregory. I know of no evidence to indicate that Yeats seriously contemplated masking actors in his own plays before 1910. And the stage-direction for the opening scene of *On Baile's Strand*, that the features of the Fool and the Blind Man are *"made grotesque and extravagant by masks,"* does not appear until 1922, when the play is reprinted in *Plays in Prose and Verse*.

masks, expressed some five years before Ezra Pound introduced him to *Noh*, partly reflects, as critics of the plays now recognize, Yeats's association with Gordon Craig; of whose stagecraft he had written enthusiastically in "At Stratford-on-Avon"; who actually designed masks for *On Baile's Strand*, as well as *The Hour-Glass*; and who, almost a decade before Yeats was to invent his new form of drama, was predicting that the mask would "in the near future" supplant the human face as a vehicle of dramatic expression.[36] Craig, apparently by independent courses, had arrived at a theory of drama close to Yeats's. As Arthur Symons had emphasized about him, in an essay surely known to Yeats, he too was reacting against the dominant naturalism of nineteenth-century English theater: decrying realistic scene painting, seeking to return theater to its roots in ritual, proposing to restore dance as a vital dramatic mode.[37] In 1905—once more, a decade before Yeats was to embark on *At the Hawk's Well*—Craig was insisting that "the father of the dramatist was the dancer," and equating poetic action with dance.[38] Two years later, in his famous essay, "The Actor and the Über-Marionette," he was to recommend that actors simulate the movement not of people but of puppets—an idea Yeats adopts for *At the Hawk's Well*, specifying that the

---

[36] For Yeats's observation in "At Stratford-on-Avon," see *The Speaker* (May 11, 1901), 159. The mask Craig fashioned for the Blind Man of *On Baile's Strand* is pictured, with his own commentary on it, in Janet Leeper, *Edward Gordon Craig: Designs for the Theatre* (Harmondsworth, Middlesex, England: Penguin Books, 1948), p. 38. For Craig's prediction concerning the future of masks in the theater, see "The Artists of the Theatre of the Future," first published in 1907 and reprinted in *On the Art of the Theatre* (London: Heinemann, 1911), especially pp. 12–13, where he discusses the advantages of masks in acting. The most sensitive and intelligent examination of Craig's influence on Yeats is still, in my view, Ann Saddlemyer's " 'The Heroic Discipline of the Looking-Glass': W.B. Yeats's Search for Dramatic Design," *The World of W.B. Yeats*, ed. Robin Skelton and Ann Saddlemyer (Victoria, British Columbia: Adelphi Bookshop, 1965), pp. 87–103. Saddlemyer claims, I think justifiably, that Craig's influence on Yeats "can hardly be over-estimated" (p. 96).

[37] See Symons' "A New Art of the Stage" (1902, 1906) in *Studies in the Seven Arts* (London: Archibald Constable, 1906).

[38] "The Art of the Theatre: The First Dialogue," *On the Art of the Theatre*, pp. 40 and 41.

gestures of the Old Man, *"like those of the other persons in the play, suggest a marionette."*

Craig's prejudice against natural movement stems from the same assumption as Yeats's: that an artifact mirrors the psyche of its artist. This assumption he, also like Yeats, owes partly to Blake, whose observation on the creative process, "All forms are perfect in the poet's mind," Craig quotes in "The Actor and the Über-Marionette."[39] That these forms are, for Craig, most nearly embodied in marionettes implies his concept of them as images: "Descendants of a great and noble family of Images . . . made 'in the likeness of God.' "[40] Which is tantamount to saying that their maker communes with the divine; that, as Yeats might have put it, he partakes of the *Anima Mundi*. Those forms the poet brings to perfection are, to complete the statement Craig borrowed from Blake, "not abstracted or compounded from nature; they are from Imagination."

It is to accentuate the imagination as a compounder of perfect forms that Yeats in *Deirdre* (1906) injects a chorus of Musicians into his scenario. Produced at about the same time as Craig's important essays, and as the second version of Symons' piece on Craig, *Deirdre* comprises a transition of sorts from the semi-Shakespearean mode of *On Baile's Strand* to the solely Yeatsian mode of *At the Hawk's Well*. As the Musicians of *At the Hawk's Well* initiate the action by calling to the eye of the mind the scene in which Cuchulain's adventure is to unfold, the First Musician of *Deirdre* introduces the tragedy by announcing that she has "a story . . ./ That has so mixed with fable in our songs/ That all seemed fabulous" (1–3). Both opening speeches serve to alert the audience to the creative, the myth-making process itself as the focus of these plays.[41] When the Second Musician in *Deirdre* responds to the First Musician's account of the heroine's elopement by commenting that "The tale were well enough/ Had it a finish" (25–26), she is acting the role of critic. And Yeats's scenario fulfills her demand: it writes a finish

---

[39] *On the Art of the Theatre*, p. 89.

[40] *Ibid.*, p. 90.

[41] With respect to *Deirdre*, I am anticipated in this observation by Clark, *W.B. Yeats and the Theatre of Desolate Reality*, pp. 30–32.

to the story the First Musician has begun (as the fate of Cuchulain in *On Baile's Strand* writes a finish to the story the Blind Man has begun to tell the Fool).

Deirdre and Naoise self-consciously participate in writing the finish to their story. Hero and heroine constitute themselves embodiments of certain cultural ideals, figures in a myth, images in the racial consciousness of Ireland—akin to Craig's marionettes. The play Yeats made out of their love and death marks a vital step toward his ultimate conception of the stage—apparently crystallized by his discovery of *Noh* and realized dramatically in *At the Hawk's Well*—as a mirror of mind.

This is not to say that his attempts to dramatize psychic events began only in 1916, or even in 1906. As Edward Engelberg persuasively argues, the translations of Pound and Fenollosa, far from turning Yeats to a new kind of theater, confirmed him in directions he had already taken.[42] As early as 1897, he had written to Fiona MacCleod:

> My own theory of poetical or legendary drama is that it should have no realistic, or elaborate, but only a symbolic and decorative setting. A forest, for instance, should be represented by a forest pattern and not by a forest painting. One should design a scene which would be an accompaniment not a reflection of the text. . . . The acting should have an equivalent distance to that of the play from common realities. The plays might be almost, in some cases, modern mystery plays.[43]

Two years later, describing the drama he wished to arise from the Irish movement, he was to declare explicitly his hope that "we may appeal to imagination alone."[44]

Appealing to imagination alone defines the thrust of the first

---

[42] *The Vast Design*, p. 94. Engelberg cites Thomas Parkinson, "Yeats and Pound: The Illusion of Influence," *Comparative Literature*, VI (1954), 256–64, as partly anticipating his conclusions. They are in turn reiterated by Ann Saddlemyer in " 'The Heroic Discipline of the Looking-Glass'," especially pp. 101 and 103, and by John Rees Moore in *Masks of Love and Death*, p. 15.

[43] Wade, *Letters*, p. 280.   [44] *Ibid.*, p. 310.

of Yeats's plays to be performed, *The Land of Heart's Desire*, which opened at the Avenue Theatre in London on March 29, 1894.[45] The Child tempting Mary Bruin to foresake home, hearth, and husband for Faery says of her folk that "we are but obedient to the thoughts/ That drift into the mind at the wink of an eye" (394–95). They are in a sense images, dreamed into being by Mary herself. Indeed the Child's promise that she can bring Mary "Where nobody gets old and crafty and wise,/ Where nobody gets old and godly and grave,/ Where nobody gets old and bitter of tongue" (390–92) echoes Mary's own account, gleaned from the grandfather's book, of Princess Edain, who "heard/ A voice singing on a May eve like this,/ And followed, half awake, and half asleep,/ Until she came into the land of Faery,/ Where nobody gets old and godly and grave,/ Where nobody gets old and crafty and wise,/ Where nobody gets old and bitter of tongue" (45–51). She expresses Mary's only half-comprehended wish. The setting for the play—a fire-lit room with an open door, through which the audience sees *"a vague, mysterious world"*—comprises a psychic metaphor. Ranged in the light around the hearth are embodiments of the restrictions and responsibilities stifling Mary's spirit: Bridget, worn to bitterness by a life of housekeeping; Maurteen, valuing only the material comforts his labor has earned; Father Hart, demanding obedience to a repressive dogma; Shawn, offering a love doomed by mortality. Hidden by the darkness beyond lies the fulfillment of Mary's dream wish, the Land of Heart's Desire itself, "Where beauty has no ebb, decay no flood,/ But joy is wisdom, time an endless song" (374–75).

The Child's passage from the night outside to the light inside projects the emergence of Mary's wish into consciousness. Yeats's scenario captures dramatically the process Blake had defined as imagination: turning mental states into personified images. The play is an early attempt to do what *At the Hawk's Well* does so brilliantly: stage the mind of the artist creating his artifact.

It is to suggest this focus that Yeats has Mary reading the grandfather's book when the curtain rises. Specifying that she

[45] For the date of the performance, see Alspach, *Variorum Plays*, p. 1313.

stand by the door, where *"if she looks up she can see . . . into the wood,"* his stage-directions establish the book as an entrée into the imagination. Mary is the artist *manqué*, communing, through his work, with the real artist, the grandfather who has redacted the tales in which she immerses herself. That Maurteen evinces contempt for the grandfather's mutterings, because *"he was no judge of a dog or a horse,/ and any idle boy could blarney him"* (57–58), manifests Yeats's concern with the subversion of the heroic and imaginative world by a bourgeois ethos, also to occupy him in *The King's Threshold* and *On Baile's Strand*.

The extent of this subversion is measured by the view of history implicit in these plays. The grandfather is three generations removed from Mary. Mary, who could not have written his book and must die to enter Faery, lives in a time "remote" from the time of the audience. And the audience is wholly cut off from Faery, fails even to believe in Faery. For the audience consists largely of Maurteens, as the audience of *The King's Threshold* consists of Mayors and Chamberlains or the audience of *On Baile's Strand* of Conchubars and Blind Men.

The audience, that is, see themselves mirrored on Yeats's stage; and the image is unflattering. In *On Baile's Strand, The Green Helmet, At the Hawk's Well,* and *The Death of Cuchulain* (to cite only examples from the Cuchulain cycle) they are made to confront themselves as repositors of civilization's decay. How that decay has come about it is one of the major functions of the Cuchulain cycle to explore.

II

The Ruins of Time

In his Preface to *Cuchulain of Muirthemne* Yeats praises the Irish story-teller for understanding "as well as Blake that the ruins of time build mansions in eternity. . . ."[1] *On Baile's Strand* dramatizes the ruins of time and, to the extent that Cuchulain by fighting the waves makes a myth of himself, the building from those ruins—through the shaping hand of its playwright—of a mansion in eternity.

The play concerns history and the deterioration it traces from a golden age of Cuchulains dancing with Shape-Changers on the shore or in the wood to a leaden world of Blind Men engineering thefts from untended ovens and Conchubars subverting the free spirit to guarantee the security of their children. "Boy," Cuchulain prophetically warns his young challenger, "If I had fought my father, he'd have killed me,/ As certainly as if I had a son/ And fought with him, I should be deadly to him;/ For the old fiery fountains are far off/ And every day there is less heat o' the blood" (592–97). Generation by generation, heroic and imaginative man declines. What the future holds for its Cuchulains is foreshadowed in the cozened Fool.

For while Yeats wrestled with the problems posed by this earliest of his truly great dramas, he was already brooding on the cyclical theory of history to emerge in *A Vision* and in his later poems and plays (perhaps, as Skene suggests, adumbrated in *On Baile's Strand* by the wheel of love and hate),[2] and moving toward the conviction that his culture was riding the downward arc of the cycle. In an essay entitled "First Principles," published in *Samhain* for 1904, as he was beginning his crucial revision of *On Baile's Strand*, he projects civilization in human form: coming briefly into beauty and strength; and weaving from that beauty and strength, even as they imperceptibly wane, a kind of order; "until in the end it lies there with its

[1] *Explorations*, p. 9.
[2] *The Cuchulain Plays of W.B. Yeats*, p. 178.

21

limbs straightened out and a clean cloth folded upon it." To this funereal image, Yeats adds, however, that "we need not follow among the mourners, for, it may be, before they are at the tomb, a messenger will run out of the hills and touch the pale lips with a red ember, and wake the limbs to the disorder and the tumult that is life. Though he does not come, even so we will keep from among the mourners and hold some cheerful conversation among ourselves; for has not Virgil, a knowledgeable man and a wizard, foretold that other Argonauts shall row between cliff and cliff, and other fair-haired Achaeans sack another Troy?"[3] The rhetorical question, through which Yeats, appealing to the authority of Virgil, manages not quite to announce himself a believer in cycles of history, looks forward to his image, wrought years later for "Lapis Lazuli," of the parade of epochs constituting history:

> On their own feet they came, or on shipboard,
> Camel-back, horse-back, ass-back, mule-back,
> Old civilisations put to the sword.
>
> (25–27)[4]

And it precisely anticipates the opening song of *The Resurrection*, which, published in *The Adelphi* for June, 1927 and initially performed at the Abbey on July 30, 1934, is roughly contemporary with "Lapis Lazuli":

> Another Troy must rise and set,
> Another lineage feed the crow,
> Another Argo's painted prow
> Drive to a flashier bauble yet.
>
> (9–12)

Both poem and play depict history, in traditional Yeatsian manner, as a recurrent cycle. Gaiety becomes, in effect, a morally obligatory stance to the poet of "Lapis Lazuli" because "All things fall and are built again,/ And those that build them again are gay" (35–36). Celebration of man's creative power is the

[3] *Explorations*, p. 150.

[4] Quotations and line references to Yeats's poems are from *The Variorum Edition of the Poems of W.B. Yeats*, ed. Peter Allt and Russell K. Alspach (New York: Macmillan, 1966).

note on which the Musicians of *The Resurrection* end their curtain song because they know—as Hebrew, Greek, and Syrian do not—that, though "Everything that man esteems/ Endures a moment or a day" (414–15), he is from the wreck of the old forever fashioning new moments, new days, fed by his own resinous heart.

The use of Musicians in plays like *The Resurrection*, or in *Deirdre* and the later Cuchulain dramas, *At the Hawk's Well* and *The Only Jealousy of Emer*, marks a variation on a technique actually, if quite differently, introduced in *On Baile's Strand*. Leonard E. Nathan proposes that Yeats invented the Blind Man and Fool to do for *On Baile's Strand* what, Yeats had himself argued in "Emotion of Multitude" (1903), the Greek chorus and Shakespearean subplot do for their plays: join "the little limited life of the fable, which is always better the simpler it is, and the rich, far-wandering, many-imaged life of the half-seen world beyond it."[5] Yeats was seeking a vehicle for inviting the audience, as the Musicians invite the audience of *At the Hawk's Well*, to participate psychically in the action. As he observes, again of the Shakespearean subplot in "Emotion of Multitude," "very commonly . . . [it] is the main plot working itself out in more ordinary men and women, and so doubly calling up before us the image of multitude."[6]

The Blind Man and Fool are, however, no mere choric voices; and as principals in a Yeatsian subplot, they mediate between actors and audience in an especially crucial way: reaching across time as well as space, forcing us to recognize in the mythic giants they shadow an age vastly superior to our own. Which is why they frame the action. The Blind Man's absorption in the benefits to be reaped from untended ovens, even in the face of the awesome tragedy unfolding before them and narrated to him by the Fool, bespeaks the moral and imaginative bankruptcy—for Yeats they come to the same thing—afflicting modern man.

[5] Nathan quotes this passage in fragmented form in *The Tragic Drama of William Butler Yeats*, p. 83. For the passage in its proper context, see *Essays and Introductions*, p. 216.

[6] *Essays and Introductions*, p. 216.

The Blind Man's blindness (reversing the symbolic use to which blindness is later to be put in "The Tower") manifests his inability to apprehend other than sensuously, to comprehend other than empirically. "I would never be able to steal anything," says the Fool, conceding that the Blind Man grasps more of the material world than he despite his eyes, "if you didn't tell me where to look for it" (4–6). And while he recounts, all but to himself, his flirtations with the witches pursuing him for a kiss, his companion gropes at Conchubar's seat, discerning through the intelligence of his fingers not alone the identity of the object but the whole course of events leading to Cuchulain's entrapment in the oath:

> *Blind Man [feeling legs of big chair with his hands].* Ah!
> [*Then, in a louder voice as he feels the back of it.*]
> Ah—ah—
> *Fool.* Why do you say 'Ah-ah'?
> *Blind Man.* I know the big chair. It is to-day the High King
>   Conchubar is coming. They have brought out his chair. He
>   is going to be Cuchulain's master in earnest from this day
>   out. It is that he's coming for.
> *Fool.* He must be a great man to be Cuchulain's master.
> *Blind Man.* So he is. He is a great man. He is over all the rest
>   of the kings in Ireland.
> *Fool.* Cuchulain's master! I thought Cuchulain could do any-
>   thing he liked.
> *Blind Man.* So he did, so he did. But he ran too wild, and
>   Conchubar is coming to-day to put an oath upon him that
>   will stop his rambling and make him as biddable as a
>   house-dog and keep him always at his hand. He will sit in
>   this chair and put the oath upon him.
>
> (35–54)

That the Blind Man is meant, in contrast to the Fool, to show a certain mastery over the material world is underscored by Yeats's recasting of this scene. In its original version the Blind Man (Fintain) must rely on the Fool (Barach) to interpret his impressions:

Fintain. [*Who has been feeling about with his stick.*] What's
    this and this?
Barach. They are chairs.
Fintain. And this?
Barach. Why, that's a bench.
Fintain. And this?
Barach. A big chair.

(18–24)

It is arguable that Yeats rewrote this dialogue first to give it
greater economy, thus increasing its dramatic impact, and only
second to clarify the symbolic function of his Blind Man. From
the perspective of the audience, Barach's answers are redun-
dant. The audience sees the furniture on stage even if, by the
situation obtaining in Cuchulain's great hall at Dundealgan,
Fintain does not.

But Yeats also, in what could not have been intended as a
mere rhetorical measure, shifts the impetus for the essential
exposition in the play—the account of the Young Man's
landing—from the Fool to the Blind Man. In the original
scenario it is Barach hiding in a ditch who witnesses the Young
Man's rout of the guardians on the shore. In the scenario revised it is the Blind Man lying in a hole and overhearing the
survivors, who reports his victory. In *On Baile's Strand* as
Yeats wished it preserved, then, the entire background of the
action is supplied by the Blind Man, who—gleaning details
through hands, ears, and, to the extent that he draws from his
sojourn in Aoife's country before losing his sight, eyes—
reflects the attunement of the material world to the senses.

That attunement to the senses implies, in such a world, resistance to the imagination is dramatized through Conchubar's
subdual of Cuchulain, and adumbrated through the Blind
Man's deception—using data gathered by the senses—of the
Fool. That the Fool, who lives mainly in imagination, finds
himself unable to cope with the problems of subsisting in this
world is stressed again by Yeats's revision of his scenario. The
Fool opens the original, announcing that he will shut the door
to keep the wind out of his bones and the Shape-Changers out

of the house. He opens the final version, praising the Blind Man
for his cleverness and looking forward to the savory fowl he has
stolen at the Blind Man's direction. By so altering this scene,
Yeats strengthens the degree to which the subplot serves as a
framing device for the play, as a statement of the imaginative
man's envelopment in the abasing selfhood of Conchubars and
Blind Men. *On Baile's Strand* in 1906 begins and ends on the
same note: as the Fool initiates the action, marvelling that none
but the Blind Man "could have thought that the henwife sleeps
every day a little at noon" (3–4), the Blind Man closes it, urging the Fool to hurry because "The ovens will be full" (803) and
no one in the houses.

The Fool of 1906, moreover, welcomes the witches he had
shut out in 1901: "Wait a minute. I shouldn't have closed the
door. There are some that look for me, and I wouldn't like them
not to find me" (20–23). Through revision, that is, Yeats
clarifies the nature of the Fool, as he clarifies the nature of the
Blind Man. For the Fool is foolish not alone because he allows
himself to be cheated of dinner by his opportunistic companion
but because he, like Cuchulain, consorts with witches. He is
foolish to practical men, for whom witches are idle tales, in the
eyes of blind men because he believes in imagination.

He is a fool as Cuchulain in *At the Hawk's Well* is an idiot.
And Cuchulain in *At the Hawk's Well* is an idiot only by the
standards of the Old Man, wishing to live "all his days/ Where a
hand on the bell/ Can call the milch cows/ To the comfortable
door of his house" (267–70). The Fool in *On Baile's Strand* is
foolish chiefly by the standards of the bourgeois world embodied in the Blind Man.

Both Nathan and Desai find in *King Lear* a source for the
complex irony attached to these labels.[7] Yeats enriches their
significance, however, through a manipulation of symbolic de-
tail drawn not from Shakespeare but from Romanticism and his
own mythic heritage. Blinded for putting a curse upon the
wind, the Blind Man looks forward to the Old Man in *At the
Hawk's Well*, who adjudges the wind "stupid" (114), and back

---

[7] See *The Tragic Drama of William Butler Yeats*, p. 84 and *Yeats's Shakespeare*, p. 15.

to Maurteen in *The Land of Heart's Desire*, who dismisses Mary's report of the Child taking the quicken wood as, like her other visions, "nothing but a puff of wind" (103). Yeats is exploiting the ancient folk tradition that the *Sidhe* ride the wind. He is also evoking the Romantic correspondence between the wind and the imagination at work. The Child in *The Land of Heart's Desire* runs "up out of the wind" (98), as the witches pursuing the Fool enter the house with the wind. Cuchulain in *At the Hawk's Well* is driven to Aoife's shore by "a lucky wind" (92). Cuchulain in *On Baile's Strand* hears his fancy compared to "a swallow on the wind" (345).

The comparison is Conchubar's, and is meant pejoratively. Impelled by the bourgeois need to perpetuate name and fame through property—to "leave/ A strong and settled country to [his] children" (214–15)—he demands order, "government" (247); and order, as Yeats knew, in part from his reading of Blake, inhibits imagination; for imagination, actuated in Cuchulain, "[mocks] at every reasonable hope,/ And would have nothing, or impossible things" (287–88).

The judgment, again, is Conchubar's; and the operative word is, from his point of view, "reasonable." "Reason," Blake has his Devil proclaim in *The Marriage of Heaven and Hell*, "is the bound or outward circumference of Energy" (4.2).[8] Cuchulain before taking the oath embodies unrestrained Energy. What is at stake in Conchubar's insistence that Cuchulain take the oath is whether he will, to use the phrase Yeats uses, perhaps directly echoing Blake, "be bound." In the Preludium to *Europe* the Blakean narrator, recasting that aphorism from *The Marriage* as an image of the new-born Christ, asks: "who shall bind the infinite with an eternal band?" (2.13). In the prophecy itself Los invites Christ's revolutionary surrogate, Orc, to rise from his deep den, "For now [with the divine birth] thou art bound" (4.13).

Cuchulain is a kind of Yeatsian Orc, a rebel against government. To Conchubar's accusation that the Young Man "came to land/ While you were somewhere out of sight and hearing,/

---

[8] Quotations from Blake are cited, from the Erdman edition, by plate and line or, in the case of *The Marriage*, by statement number.

Hunting or dancing with your wild companions," Cuchulain responds that "I'll not be bound" (207–10). To Cuchulain's apparent unconcern at the dangers besetting Ulster, Conchubar responds by pleading that old counsellors and young kings together "Are held . . . by the one anxiety./ Will you be bound into obedience . . .?" (350–51). Of the lines the Women chant to accompany Cuchulain's pledge, Conchubar explains that "Considering/ That the wild will of man could be oath-bound,/ But that a woman's could not, they bid us sing/ Against the will of women at its wildest. . . ." (388–91). When, with the ceremony completed, the Young Man's knock is heard, Conchubar orders the door opened, "for I would have all know/ That the oath's finished and Cuchulain bound. . . ." (454–55).

Conchubar's aims in binding Cuchulain are pragmatic, acquisitive, amenable to moral compromise. Cuchulain's aims in resisting Conchubar are infinite. The ultimate consequence of Conchubar's ethos is acted out by the Blind Man reaching into untended ovens.

The spiritual kinship of Conchubar and the Blind Man is mirrored in the view they share of Cuchulain's conduct. The Blind Man tells the Fool that Conchubar is to impose the oath on Cuchulain because "he ran too wild" (49). Conchubar himself characterizes Cuchulain as possessing "wildness of . . . blood" (244), and sees in the oath an instrument for curbing man's "wild will" (389). That this view prevails not alone with their countrymen but with Cuchulain as well affirms the inevitability of the hero's demise. In *Europe* Los discovers that Energy, even destructive Energy, cannot be bound:

> . . . terrible Orc, when he beheld the morning in the east,
> Shot from the heights of Enitharmon;
> And in the vineyards of red France appear'd the light of his
> fury.
>
> (14.37–15.2)

In *On Baile's Strand* Energy submits to being bound, in effect to being destroyed. The ultimate consequence of Cuchulain's ethos is thus acted out in his fight with the sea. If impossible things are, as Conchubar implies, truly impossible, nothing is the sole choice left.

To make less than this choice between absolutes is to be, by Yeats's standards, a fool—like the Blind Man. The Fool himself turns from Cuchulain's awesome struggle to participate in the Blind Man's thievery. Accepting the symbiotic relation to his corrupter that his heroic alter-ego had affirmed by oath, then repudiated—"I give my wisdom," says Conchubar, "and I take your strength" (446)—the Fool comes in the end to act out the abasement of the imaginative man. By "take," Yeats, speaking through Conchubar, means "drain" as well as "gain." And Yeats's belief that the course of history renders this drain inevitable is partly what dictates his removal from the stage of the climactic heroism expressing Cuchulain's repudiation, that it be filtered through the bedazzled eyes of the hero's caricature self.

Framing the play's serious action with a parodic subplot mirrors the subversive effect on the world of the atrophy afflicting imagination. Through the oath Conchubar imposes on Cuchulain, imagination is ritually degraded. As the Fool awaiting his dinner opens the door of the assembly house to the witches, Conchubar awaiting Cuchulain's assent to the oath orders the door shut to keep the witches out.

The door, as in *The Land of Heart's Desire*, symbolizes man's access to his unconscious, and so to the *Anima Mundi*. In "Magic," which Yeats was ruminating and writing even as *On Baile's Strand* began to take form, he transfers into an expository context the entire setting of house, hearth, and door specifically to lament urban man's insulation from that other world:

> We cannot doubt that barbaric people receive such influences more easily and fully than we do, for our life in cities, which deafens or kills the passive meditative life, and our education that enlarges the separated, self-moving mind, have made our souls less sensitive. Our souls that were once naked to the winds of heaven are now thickly clad, and have learned to build a house and light a fire upon its hearth, and shut-to the doors and windows.[9]

The stage-directions to *On Baile's Strand* call for this same dichotomy between the comfortable domestic arrangements of

---

[9] *Essays and Introductions*, p. 41.

an interior scene and a mysterious beyond, dimly spied through the door as *"misty light as of sea-mist."*

The Fool and Cuchulain, welcoming what passes the door, like Mary in *The Land of Heart's Desire*, are poets *manqués*. Cuchulain displays a kind of aesthetic sensibility: he objects to sitting at the council-board "Among the unshapely bodies of old men" (219). His metaphorical, if not mythological, identification with the sun against the moon—made explicit by Yeats in his oft-quoted question to Frank Fay, "are they [Conchubar and Cuchulain] not the cold moon and the hot sun?"[10]—is meant to underscore this aspect of Cuchulain's nature. For Yeats, justifying the correspondence by his reading of Blake and Shelley, had in 1904 (the date of his letter to Fay) associated imagination with the sun rather than the moon. "The Sun," he declares in "The Philosophy of Shelley's Poetry," "is the symbol of sensitive life, and of belief and joy and pride and energy, of indeed the whole life of the will, and of that beauty which neither lures from far off, nor becomes beautiful in giving itself, but makes all glad because it is beauty." And he concludes it "therefore natural that Blake, who was always praising energy, and all exalted overflowing of oneself, and who thought art an impassioned labour to keep man from doubt and despondency, and women's love an evil, when it would trammel man's will, should see the poetic genius not in a woman star but in the Sun, and should rejoice throughout his poetry in 'the Sun in his strength.' "[11] The witches who, by tempting Cuchulain as well as the Fool would thwart the kind of women's love trammeling man's will, are thus Muse figures—species of those mental images or apparitions Yeats in *Per Amica Silentia Lunae* reports discovering in the *Anima Mundi*. As the Fool tells the Blind Man, "They come by in the wind" (26)—like the faery folk drawing Mary Bruin. They also emerge from the sea—like Fand in *The Only Jealousy of Emer*, who, *"more an idol than a human being,"* Yeats's stage-directions specify, seems all but an artifact.

[10] Wade, *Letters*, p. 425.
[11] *Essays and Introductions*, p. 93.

The sea repeatedly serves Yeats, as Thomas R. Whitaker among others has pointed out, to image the *Anima Mundi*. Whitaker's example is "Rosa Alchemica."[12] Yeats suggests the same analogy, however, in another, later prose piece more directly germane to *On Baile's Strand*, and to his subsequent Cuchulain plays, "The Tragic Theatre," where he asserts that in the face of great tragedy "We feel our minds expand convulsively or spread out slowly like some moon-brightened image-crowded sea."[13] And he makes the analogy explicit in *Per Amica*, where he depicts the "daily thought" of himself and his predecessors in investigating the world beyond consciousness as "certainly but the line of foam at the shallow edge of a vast luminous sea; Henry More's *Anima Mundi*, Wordsworth's 'immortal sea which brought us hither . . . and near whose edge children sport,' . . ."[14]

The Yeatsian attitude underlying his recurrence to this constellation of imagery—house, hearth, door, wind, and sea—informs the scene of the oath-taking, with its chorus of Women intoning the values of those whose love would trammel man's will and invoking the spirits of threshold and hearthstone to "drive/ The Women none can kiss and thrive,/ For they are but whirling wind,/ Out of memory and mind" (399–402). This choric appeal admits of two complementary readings. While the singers call on their domestic gods to exorcise the Shape-Changers, because in tempting the men of Ulster to seek possession of what is unpossessible, but whirling wind, they debilitate them, Yeats, speaking through the singers, identifies the Shape-Changers as creatures of imagination—"Out of memory and mind." The man the choric song evokes to epitomize the fate of those pursued by witches—"Emptied, ruined, wracked, and lost,/ . . . for at most/ They will give him kiss for kiss" (419–21)—re-enacts the situation of the Fool. And the Fool impatient for his dinner—his teeth, he tells the Blind Man, "growing long with the hunger" (75)—is a lesser version of

[12] *Swan and Shadow: Yeats's Dialogue with History* (Chapel Hill: The University of North Carolina Press, 1959), p. 40.

[13] *Essays and Introductions*, p. 245.

[14] *Per Amica Silentia Lunae*, p. 63.

Cuchulain, in the role enjoined on him by his murder of Culain the smith's watchdog, as Hound of Culain.[15]

Cuchulain, his surrogate, all men held in thrall by these Celtic variants on *La Belle Dame Sans Merci* suffer as both hunter hound and hunted hind. Evoking Actaeon, torn to pieces for spying Diana in her bath, or the hornless deer chased eternally by a phantom hound encountered by Oisin in his wanderings, the singers warn of the witches that "They would change them into hounds/ Until he had died of his wounds,/ . . . Or they'd hurl a spell at him,/ That he follow with desire/ Bodies that can never tire/ Or grow kind. . . ." (407–13). And the series of torments the singers recount, ascending in intensity to the exchange of kiss for kiss, has as its ultimate psychic consequence that, "After this," in words the singers attribute to the witches themselves, "Hatred may be sweet to the taste" (422–23). Their song foreshadows the destiny of Cuchulain, who in *At the Hawk's Well* (postdating *On Baile's Strand* in composition though predating it in the sequence of events) is warned by the Old Man that to gaze into the Guardian's unmoistened eyes is to be cursed—

> That curse may be
> Never to win a woman's love and keep it;
> Or always to mix hatred in the love;
> Or it may be that she will kill your children,
> That you will find them, their throats torn and bloody,
> Or you will be so maddened that you kill them
> With your own hand.
>
> (173–79)

—and who in *On Baile's Strand* itself, cozened by Conchubar as the Fool by the Blind Man, assaulted by Aoife's love turned hate, in fact kills his child with his own hand.

Rendering the Muse a cruel, destructive mistress—*La Belle Dame* leaving the knight haggard and woebegone—constitutes

---

[15] See "Boy Deeds of Cuchulain" in *Cuchulain of Muirthemne* (New York: Oxford University Press, 1973), pp. 25–28. Skene, *Cuchulain Plays*, p. 159, perceives in the Fool's hunger a mirror of Cuchulain's "doom-eager" passion, but ignores its hound-like quality.

one of the enduring traditions Yeats inherited from his Romantic precursors.[16] If Cuchulain in *At the Hawk's Well* is cursed by gazing into the Guardian's unmoistened eyes, Cuchulain in *The Only Jealousy of Emer* is wooed to the brink of death by Fand, and awakens gripped by a fear he cannot explain. The Swineherd and Stroller of *A Full Moon in March* and *The King of the Great Clock Tower* must lose their heads to have their will of the wintry Queen.

And the Fool, because he is not Cuchulain but a reduction of Cuchulain, repudiates the quest entirely. Where Cuchulain pursues his tormentors, real or imagined, even into the waves, the Fool renounces them to protect his share in the stolen chicken: "we won't give them any of the fowl. Let them go back to the sea, let them go back to the sea" (32–34). He is repressing his own desires, turning from them finally to embrace the Blind Man's materialism; rejecting, as the true poet never can, his idealized image of himself, what Yeats would call his anti-self.

For the Cuchulain he perceives is, to a degree, his invention, a figure in the song, "He has killed kings," into which the Fool breaks anticipating Cuchulain's entrance, and which Yeats added between 1904 and 1906 as part of his sweeping revision of the play. Yeats altered no play in his canon (unless perhaps *The Player Queen*) more fundamentally than *On Baile's Strand*, and the changes he made push the scenario toward psychodrama, toward a setting in the deeps of the mind.

That the Fool's song establishes Cuchulain as in one sense a figure in the deeps of the singer's mind is manifest through the sequence of dramatic details to which the song forms a hub. Teased into curiosity by the Blind Man's claim to know the father of the youth who has routed the guardians of the shore, the Fool decides that he will, then that he dares not ask Cuchulain: "I'll ask him. Cuchulain will know. He was in Aoife's country. . . . But no, I won't ask him, I would be afraid" (184–87). His vacillations culminate in a direct address to Cuchulain himself—"No, no, Cuchulain, I'm not going to ask you" (193–94)—though the hero has yet to enter the assembly

---

[16] See Harold Bloom, *Yeats*, especially pp. 53, 150, 232, and 266.

house. And the Cuchulain whom the Fool declines to ask, an image in his mind's eye, elicits a verse of the song he had earlier sung to celebrate the invincibility of his master:

> He has killed kings,
> Kings and the sons of kings,
> Dragons out of the water,
> And witches out of the air
> Banachas and Bonachas and people of the woods.
>
> (195–99)

The last words of the song are, the stage-directions specify, sung outside, blending into the voice of Cuchulain remonstrating with Conchubar as they approach the hall:

> Because I have killed men without your bidding
> And have rewarded others at my own pleasure,
> Because of a half a score of trifling things,
> You'd lay this oath upon me . . .
>
> (200–203)

This method of managing entrances and exits, essentially repeated in the appearance of the Young Man and the reappearance of the Blind Man and Fool, reflects Yeats's exploitation of the large platform without proscenium or curtain which, as Skene, citing the Preface to *Plays in Prose and Verse* (1922), notes, had at the turn of the century already become Yeats's idea of the proper stage for his theater.[17] The possibilities for turning the continuous action the platform stage encourages to ironic or symbolic effect he learned at least partly from Shakespeare and the visit to Stratford-on-Avon he made before beginning *On Baile's Strand*. Cuchulain protesting Conchubar's demand appears almost an extension of the Fool celebrating Cuchulain's battle prowess. He enters through the back door—symbolically, again, the passage between the conscious and unconscious realms of the mind—as if an image evoked by the Fool's imagination and given material being by his song. He seems, that is, an outgrowth of the song, as the action of *Deirdre* (largely written the same year the revised *On Baile's*

[17] *The Cuchulain Plays of W.B. Yeats*, p. 114.

Strand was published) seems an outgrowth of the First Musician's opening lines. The Fool and the Blind Man relate to the audience, moreover, in a way analogous not alone to the Musicians of *Deirdre* (as well as *At the Hawk's Well*) but to the Red Man of *The Green Helmet*, who in his curtain speech assumes a choric role comparable to theirs. Having catalogued the virtues earning Cuchulain the championship of the land, he concludes that they will prosper only until the day "When heart and mind shall darken that the weak may end the strong/ And the long remembering harpers have matter for their song" (282–84). The audience lives in the day of the weak's ascendancy over the strong, and Yeats writing his plays has become the long remembering harper. In *The Death of Cuchulain* he is specifically to dramatize the ending by the weak of the strong. In *On Baile's Strand* he is dramatizing the survival by the weak of the strong.

For the strong in *On Baile's Strand* ends himself—psychically, then physically. Having watched Cuchulain rush out to kill his son, the first of the three Women singers observes that "Life drifts between a fool and a blind man/ To the end, and nobody can know his end" (623–24). In her cryptic utterance is foretold the course of history. Cuchulain starts as a fool, by Conchubar's standards, and drifts toward becoming Conchubar's fool indeed, toward blindness comparable to Conchubar's own. The scenario encapsulates the world's drift from tolerating the independence, if not the hegemony, of its Cuchulains to welcoming the hegemony of its Conchubars; which is to say, the scenario prefigures the hegemony of the Blind Man and the bourgeois abasement he bespeaks.

This drift is foreshadowed in Cuchulain's lapse from complete freedom—"I'll dance or hunt, or quarrel or make love,/ Wherever and whenever I've a mind to" (211–12)—into imprisonment by the terms of the oath. The deterioration inherent in this imprisonment Cuchulain at least intuitively perceives. Resisting Conchubar's demand, he attributes it to time having "put water in your blood" (213). Acquiescing, he rationalizes that, "It's time the years put water in my blood/ And drowned the wildness of it, for all's changed,/ But that unchanged'' (376–78). In the overall scheme of the play the imagery of water and drowning anticipates Cuchulain's envelopment by the sea. Even the identity and intention of his challenger are announced, by the Blind Man, in a figure suggesting the tide: ''It flows in upon me that it is Aoife's son'' (129–30).

The water imagery also suggests a waning of the strength which—inherited by Cuchulain from his father Lugh, the sun god, and so portrayed in fire—Conchubar's children have grown to fear. In the immediate aftermath of the oath the domination of fire by water measures Cuchulain's fall toward a state akin to Conchubar's, whose blood has already thinned to water: it presages his blindness to the identity of his son. Conchubar's children entreat him to curb Cuchulain because, as Conchubar verbalizes their pleas, ''We shall be at his mercy when you are gone;/ He burns the earth if he were a fire/ And time can never touch him'' (237–39). Conchubar himself announces, as a result of Cuchulain's binding, ''that the swords are drinking up the flame'' (456). After Cuchulain's departure for the field where he will fight his son, the Second Woman invites her colleagues, in language precisely anticipating the hero's end, to ''look upon the quenching of this greatness'' (625).

In the spectrum of values underlying the play the imagery of water drowning fire thus implies Cuchulain's lapse into real folly. Skene perceptively observes that, insofar as the Fool embodies Cuchulain's spirit or imagination, his failure to ask Cuchulain about the Young Man's father is ''highly significant'';[18] by which I take it he means that the Fool's failure adumbrates Cuchulain's later, tragic failure to recognize his son. When Cuchulain returns triumphant over the Young Man, despite the Second Woman's vision of his roof-tree consumed, he uses the feathers the Fool has been putting into his hair—the Fool's sole reward for his heroism—to wipe the blood from his sword. The gesture measures Cuchulain's diminution, psychologically associating him with the Fool and metaphorically with the chicken the Fool has stolen. It measures his decline from a stature approaching his father's, symbolized by the

---

[18] *Ibid.*, p. 166.

hawk, toward the ordinariness of the young kings, whom he characterizes as "my chicks, my nestlings" (434).

Conchubar himself, ironically, sums up Cuchulain's psychic deterioration when, faced with his refusal to abide the oath and fight the stranger, he accuses him of madness. Madness is the ultimate folly; and by Conchubar's lights, madness alone can explain Cuchulain's conduct. He countenances anarchy against the High King's effort to achieve order.

But the real madness lies, as John Rees Moore suggests, in Cuchulain's repudiation of the instinct urging friendship with his challenger; in Cuchulain's belief, fostered by Conchubar, that he has been deceived by witches.[19] Attributing his affinity for the Young Man to the machinations of witches is tantamount to accepting the hostile view of them expressed in the Women's song, to rejecting them as the Fool has in wishing them back to the sea. It is tantamount to repressing the life of imagination.

The consequence of repressing imagination to the man who lives by imagination is manifest in the impact of the oath on Cuchulain. For the oath poses him with an insoluble dilemma, entrapping him between his spontaneous love of the Young Man and his sworn fealty to the High King. The ethical and spiritual implications of this dilemma are dramatized through the exchange of gifts—Cuchulain's cloak for the Young Man's arm-ring—by which their friendship is affirmed. The exchange constitutes a kind of ritual gesture, comparable to the ritual binding Cuchulain to Conchubar. Sealing the ritual of the oath, Cuchulain assures the assemblage that "I never gave a gift and took it again" (440). Yet giving a gift and taking it again are what he does when, under the delusion that he has been duped by witches, he renounces his tie to the Young Man and calls him out to battle.

That this encounter repeats by contrast the encounter of Cuchulain and his divine father, Lugh, and that in fighting his son Cuchulain is therefore departing from the wisdom of the

---

[19] See Moore's essay, "The Idea of a Yeats Play," *W.B. Yeats: Centenary Essays on the Art of W.B. Yeats*, ed. D.E.S. Maxwell and A.B. Bushrui (Ibadan, Nigeria: Ibadan University Press, 1965), p. 157.

gods, Yeats accentuated through his revision of the play. In his original scenario he had Cuchulain, offering his gift to the Young Man, say merely that "My father gave me this heavy purple cloak." In his final version he has Cuchulain add, by way of elaboration, that Lugh "came to try me, rising up at dawn/ Out of the cold dark of the rich sea./ He challenged me to battle, but before/ My sword had touched his sword, told me his name/ Gave me this cloak, and vanished" (543–47).

By revising, Yeats also made of this scene a reiteration of Conchubar's empirical and ego-ridden motives for demanding an oath and forbidding Cuchulain's friendship with the Young Man. Witnessing their growing comraderie, the Conchubar of 1903 and 1904 remains silent despite his alarm until, confronted with as it were a *fait accompli*, he remarks that "Some witch of the air has troubled Cuchulain's mind" (553). But the Conchubar of 1906 tries to interrupt their accord in process. To Cuchulain's pleasure at seeing "there's no more need for words/ And that you'll be my friend from this day out" (522–23), Conchubar (in a speech of which the original holds no hint) protests: "He has come hither not in his own name/ But in Queen Aoife's, and has challenged us/ In challenging the foremost man of us all" (524–26). And when Cuchulain asks, "Well, well, what matter?" (527), Conchubar responds angrily (again in dialogue added through revision): "You think it does not matter,/ And that a fancy lighter than the air,/ A whim of the moment, has more matter in it./ For, having none that shall reign after you,/ You cannot think as I do, who would leave/ A throne too high for insult" (527–32).

The Young Man is, moreover, also bound. He is the instrument of Aoife, the expression, in Skene's apt remark, of "woman's will at its wildest,"[20] which Yeats, again exploiting the potential for Shakespearean irony inherent in continuous action, underscores by his structuring of the Young Man's entrance. His knock and cry, "Open! open!" sound as if in answer to Cuchulain's prayer to the "pure, glittering ones" to "Give us the enduring will, the unquenchable hope,/ The friendliness of the sword!" (449 and 451–52). His appearance "*with a drawn*

[20] *The Cuchulain Plays of W.B. Yeats*, p. 183.

sword" punctuates Conchubar's self-satisfied boast that the assembled swords drink up the flame.

The Young Man's sword too drinks up the flame—not of Cuchulain's heroic energy but of the hearth. Yet because Conchubar, in effect Aoife herself, the cultural ambiance they encompass, offers Cuchulain no way of reconciling the opposed claims of loyalty to king and kingdom and love for the Young Man, he is forced to choose age over youth, the pragmatic over the heroic—to fight the fight his father had refused—and so contribute to the coming victory of the weak over the strong. He is forced to cut off his noble descent at the behest of a bourgeois dispensation: as Moore argues, to kill a part of himself, which is madness indeed.[21] The Second Woman's vision of Cuchulain's roof-tree leaping into the fire, its walls split and blackening—seemingly awry, given the outcome of the battle and his subsequent death by water—is shown to be genuinely prophetic. He is induced to turn his divinely conferred strength against the perpetuation of its own ideals, against the perpetuation of itself.

This essentially entropic condition defines for Yeats the nature of the fallen world, the intractableness of which compels the hero (as Yeats himself insists in *Per Amica Silentia Lunae*) to find and make his mask in defeat.[22] Cuchulain's defeat confronts him in the identity of his challenger. He enacts it by fighting the unconquerable tide: forsaking the world for the *Sidhe*, the imagination, *Anima Mundi*.

For in the world action betrays. Yeats accentuates its betrayal by the same sort of structural irony shaping the Young Man's entrance. The First Woman's lament at what the ashes of the bowl tell her—"there'll be need of cries/ And rending of the hair when it's all finished" (626–27)—yields, as she and her companions leave, to cries and rending of hair indeed:

> *Enter the Fool, dragging the Blind Man*
> Fool. You have eaten it, you have eaten it! You have left me
>   nothing but the bones.
> *He throws Blind Man down by big chair.*

21 "The Idea of a Yeats Play," p. 157.
22 *Per Amica Silentia Lunae*, p. 33.

Blind Man. O, that I should have to endure such a plague! O,
I ache all over! O, I am pulled to pieces! This is the way
you pay me all the good I have done you.

(628–33)

In the fullness of time the terrifying impact of Cuchulain rush-
ing out to fight his own son shrinks to the dimensions of a
squabble between a fool and a blind man.

Such is the world's betrayal and Cuchulain's tragedy.
Through death, therefore, he symbolically abandons action for
reverie. Yeats's concept of reverie derives in part from his reading of Shelley, whose observation in "On Life," that "Those
who are subject to the state called reverie feel as if their nature
were resolved into the surrounding universe or as if the surrounding universe were resolved into their being," he quotes
with approval in "The Philosophy of Shelley's Poetry." He
then comments on the observation that Shelley himself "must
have expected to receive thoughts and images from beyond his
own mind, just in so far as that mind transcended its preoccupa-
tion with particular time and place, for he believed inspiration a
kind of death. . . ."[23]

Believing inspiration a kind of death renders art a perilous
undertaking for the artist. And construing art a perilous undertaking leads Yeats, as it had led Shelley, to a form positing the
artist as his own hero in what Harold Bloom rightly labels internalized quest romance.[24] It is this form toward which Yeats
is building in his decision to remove the actual fight with the sea
from the stage, to have the Fool narrate it not only to the Blind
Man but also to the audience. To have the Fool narrate Cuchulain's ordeal is to turn Cuchulain himself, as he had earlier been
turned by the Fool's song, into an image in the Fool's mind, to
turn the fight into a tale the Fool tells.

As a dramatic strategy, this device may well have recom-
mended itself to Yeats through its use by Robert Bridges in the
climactic scene of *The Return of Ulysses,* which he admired
immensely. In March, 1897, he had written to Bridges:

[23] *Essays and Introductions,* pp. 79–80.
[24] *Yeats,* pp. 3–4.

I read the end of the *Ulysses* with the utmost excitement. You have held a clear mirror to the magnificent rush of the greatest of all poetry, the end of the Odyssey. It would be a fine thing on the stage and should get there in time.[25]

Three months later he was reiterating his enthusiasm in print, asserting that Bridges in *The Return of Ulysses* exemplifies Maeterlinck's view of the stance appropriate to the true artist, who " 'no longer chooses Marius triumphing over the Cimbrians, or the assassination of the Duke of Guise, as fit subjects for his art; for he is well aware that the psychology of victory or murder is but elementary and exceptional, and that the solemn voice of men and things, the voice that issues forth so timidly and hesitatingly, cannot be heard amidst the idle uproar of acts of violence. And therefore will he place on his canvas a house lost in the heart of the country, a door open at the end of a passage, a face or hands at rest.' "[26]

Maeterlinck's idea of the proper setting for art—that country house with its open door—approximates the setting of *On Baile's Strand*. And Yeats's comment on Maeterlinck suggests much of the intention behind the play's final scene:

I do not understand him to mean that our dramas should have no victories or murders, for he quotes for our example plays that have both, but only that their victories and murders shall not be to excite our nerves, but to illustrate the reveries of a wisdom which shall be as much a part of the daily life of the wise as a face or hands at rest.[27]

Yeats cites as a consummate instance of such reverie achieved on the stage Bridges' treatment of Ulysses slaughtering the suitors, which, like Cuchulain fighting the sea, is not dramatized but narrated by Penelope's maid.

Attesting in his review to how deeply he was himself moved

[25] Wade, *Letters*, p. 281.
[26] See "The Return of Ulysses," *Essays and Introductions*, p. 198. Yeats's review of Bridges' play originally appeared in *The Bookman* for June, 1897 as "Mr. Robert Bridges."
[27] *Ibid.*, p. 198.

by this scene, Yeats echoes with some elaboration the praise he
had volunteered in his letter to Bridges:

> As I read, the gathering passion overwhelms me, as it did
> when Homer himself was the singer, and when I read at last
> the lines in which the maid describes to Penelope the battle
> with the suitors, at which she looks through the open door, I
> tremble with excitement.[28]

In *On Baile's Strand* Yeats imitates Bridges and goes him one
better. The Fool not only looks through the door to describe
Cuchulain's combat but, absorbed into what he sees, acts out
the response Yeats hopes to elicit from his audience. He too is
overwhelmed, at least momentarily, by gathering passion; he
too trembles with excitement. When the Blind Man tries to
turn his attention from Cuchulain to the empty houses, the
Fool at first fails to hear him:

> *Blind Man.* You say they are running out of the houses?
>   There will be nobody left in the houses. Listen, Fool!
> *Fool.* There, he is down! He is up again. He is going out in
>   the deep water. There is a big wave. It has gone over him. I
>   cannot see him now. He has killed kings and giants, but
>   the waves have mastered him, the waves have mastered
>   him!
> *Blind Man.* Come here, Fool!
> *Fool.* The waves have mastered him.
> *Blind Man.* Come here!
> *Fool.* The waves have mastered him.
>
>   (789–99)

The Fool, however briefly, transcends himself as thief and beggar manipulated by the Blind Man to become participant in and
poet of Cuchulain's tragedy. The language and rhythm to
which he rises in describing the spectacle before him—"He has
killed kings and giants"—recalls the language and rhythm of
the song he sings at Cuchulain's entrance. It resolves into the
all but hypnotic repetition, "The waves have mastered him."
    The Fool's absorption in Cuchulain's mastery by the waves,

[28] *Ibid.*, p. 199.

expressed through his repetition of that single utterance, suggests Yeats's idea of the purpose of rhythm in verse, which, he claims in "The Symbolism of Poetry," "is to prolong the moment of contemplation, the moment when we are both asleep and awake, which is the one moment of creation, by hushing us with an alluring monotony, while it holds us waking by variety, to keep us in that state of perhaps real trance, in which the mind liberated from the pressure of the will is unfolded in symbols."[29] That the Blind Man ultimately succeeds in breaking the Fool's contemplation, in wrenching him back into the world of empty houses and full ovens, reflects the fragility of the creative moment before the pressure of will. That the Fool ascends to such a moment at all, even in the face of the Blind Man's insistent opportunism, implies its potential as a defense against the abasing, materialistic will. In *On Baile's Strand* the moment proves brief, and seems in the end forever lost. At almost the same time as this play was appearing in its final form, however, Yeats was gestating a new play, *Deirdre*, in which prolonging the moment would itself comprise the dramatic experience, and, through the medium of Musicians, the audience would be invited to share in the process with the playwright.

[29] *Essays and Introductions*, p. 159.

III

Getting the Story Right

"Art," Yeats wrote in "The Play, the Player, and the Scene," from *Samhain* for 1904, "delights in the exception, for it delights in the soul expressing itself according to its own laws and arranging the world about it in its own pattern, as sand strewn upon a drum will change itself into different patterns, according to the notes of music that are sung or played to it."[1] Essentially a polemic for the kind of drama Yeats hoped to bring to the Abbey, this statement all but proclaims *On Baile's Strand* the archetypal modern tragedy. *On Baile's Strand* concerns the fate of a soul struggling, against determined resistance by the world, to express itself according to its own laws. Indeed, Yeats had opined to Lady Gregory, also in 1904, that the play was the best he had written.[2]

That he nonetheless grew dissatisfied with it is suggested not only by his sweeping revisions but by *Deirdre*, which attests to a change in his approach to dramatic form. What Yeats had emphasized to Lady Gregory about *On Baile's Strand* was its ending, which he found "particularly impressive." Its impressiveness to him reflects his feeling, at least for the moment, that in it he had solved a problem vexing him from his first attempts at drama: how to portray the exception in which art delights without, by embodying it in a human actor speaking before a human audience, reducing it to the unexceptional. In an essay entitled "The Theatre," published in *The Dome* for April, 1899, Yeats had argued that "Even if poetry were spoken as poetry, it would still seem out of place in many of its highest moments upon a stage where the superficial appearances of nature are so closely copied; for poetry is founded upon convention, and becomes incredible the moment painting or gesture reminds us that people do not speak verse when they meet upon the highway." From this observation, he concludes that "The theatre of art, when it comes to exist [and which Yeats was striving to create], must

---

[1] *Explorations*, p. 168. [2] Wade, *Letters*, p. 444.

. . . discover grave and decorative gesture, such as delighted Rossetti or Madox Brown, and grave and decorative scenery that will be forgotten the moment an actor has said, 'It is dawn,' or 'It is raining,' or 'The wind is shaking the trees'; and dresses of so little irrelevant magnificence that the mortal actors and actresses may change without much labour into the immortal people of romance." Only through such an aggressive anti-realistic program, Yeats theorizes, can theater be restored to its greatness; which, for him, means returning it to its roots in ritual, "recalling words to their ancient sovereignty."[3]

Yeats is to find his ultimate design for recalling words to their ancient sovereignty in *At the Hawk's Well*, replacing scene painting with choric description and props with geometric shapes. He had taken a significant step toward this design in *On Baile's Strand*, removing Cuchulain's apotheosis from the stage, projecting it through the eyes of the Fool. He takes another in *Deirdre*, making the whole play the finish the Second Musician asks of the story begun by the First Musician.

In *Deirdre* he felt that, as he asserts in his Preface to *Plays for an Irish Theatre*, he had at last written a play capable of realizing the ends of tragic art, which "moves us by setting us to reverie, by alluring us almost to the intensity of trance." Setting us to reverie he defines, repeating his formulation from "The Tragic Theatre," as, again, drowning dykes, inducing our minds to "expand convulsively or spread out slowly like some moon-brightened image-crowded sea." Thus, he avers, "When I am watching my own *Deirdre* I am content with the players and myself, if I am moved for a while not by the contrasted sorrows of Deirdre and Naisi, but because the words have called up before me the image of the sea-born woman so distinctively that Deirdre seems by contrast to those unshaken eyelids that had but the sea's cold blood what I had wished her to seem, a wild bird in a cage."[4] The figures in conflict on the stage are less important than the figures evoked by words and held in the mind's eye. The test of the play consists in its potential for establishing that communion between playwright and audience enabling the audience to share in the playwright's creative experience.

[3] *Essays and Introductions*, pp. 169–70.   [4] *Variorum Plays*, pp. 1298–99.

Deirdre dramatizes the making of its own myth, in effect the process culminating in the play itself. Behind it lies Yeats's understanding of how words get recalled to their ancient sovereignty. In this sense the tale of Lugaidh Redstripe and his lady is crucial. Their conduct enacts the law Naoise wishes to affirm in himself and Deirdre. They anticipate the hero in *The Death of Cuchulain* declaring to his servant, "I make the truth!" (84). And the power to make truth not only persists as an index to the nature of heroic character in the Cuchulain cycle but extends to protagonists throughout Yeats's plays. The Swineherd of *A Full Moon in March* first draws the Queen into participating in the telling of his story "of a woman . . . all bathed in blood" (116–17), then induces her to participate in the story indeed. The Boy of *Purgatory* sees the groom in the window after the Old Man, by his narration, has imprinted the image on his mind.

Purgatory, of course, also measures the limits of human power to make truth. The Old Man cannot redeem his mother or himself from their suffering. The Swineherd wins his Queen only by losing his head. Cuchulain fulfills his heroic nature ultimately by losing his. Deirdre and Naoise make their myth, even if not as Lugaidh Redstripe and his lady make theirs, by meeting the same fate. Each of them nonetheless reflects the Yeatsian dogma that hero and artist are impelled by like sensibilities. Cuchulain's awareness that he, by his actions, makes truth is akin to Deirdre's, when she gives her bracelet to the First Musician "To show that you have Deirdre's story right" (535). The identity of myth and truth is perceived by hero and artist alone—in this play by Deirdre (after anguished struggle), by Naoise, and by the Musicians. To Fergus, the Musicians purvey merely "wild thought/ Fed on extravagant poetry, and lit/ By such a dazzle of old fabulous tales/ That common things are lost, and all that's strange/ Is true because 'twere pity if it were not" (106–10).

Yeats, it would seem, is staging the conflict of Guaire and Seanchan, or of the Blind Man and Fool, Conchubar and Cuchulain over again. But he is doing it with a difference. Neither cynicism nor self-interest motivates Fergus. He proves receptive to Conchubar's treachery and impervious to the truths embedded in poetry because, to apply a phrase Yeats uses elsewhere, he lacks a vision of evil. "I have," Fergus insists, rejecting the Musicians' warning, "believed the best of every man,/ And find that to believe it is enough/ To make a bad man show him at his best,/ Or even a good man swing his lantern higher" (223–26). This naiveté is what leads him to mistake the signs—the dark-faced men outside the doors and windows, the absence of a messenger from Conchubar—and to shrug off the menace Naoise reads into the chessboard, left from the betrayal of Lugaidh Redstripe and his lady: "it were best forgot" (185).

Dismissing their murder as best forgotten specifies the consequences of Fergus' myopia. It repeats his characterization of the past evoked by the Musicians as "not worth remembering" (116) and his hasty withdrawal of the suggestion that they sing to Naoise and Deirdre of Lugaidh Redstripe: "no, not him,/ He and his lady perished wretchedly" (119–20). Finally, it manifests in another form his refusal to hear the First Musician's report of the bridal chamber being prepared in Conchubar's house: "Be silent, or I'll drive you from the door" (98).

Fergus is demanding silence of the voice of poetry itself. In so doing he is repressing part of his own nature. Though he justifies his rebuke to the Musicians by his claim to know Conchubar's mind "as if it were my own" (103), his spontaneous request for the tale of Lugaidh Redstripe implies that he knows Conchubar's mind better than he realizes. He grasps at least instinctively the reality behind the appearance of things.

Yet the pragmatist and politician, as well as optimist, in him prevents recognition of what instinct reveals. When the First Musician, with a prescience all but shaping itself into a refrain for this opening scene, translates instinct into assertion—"old men are jealous"—Fergus rationalizes her wisdom away: "I am Conchubar's near friend, and that weighed somewhat,/ And it was policy to pardon them" (65–66). When Fergus is faced with evidence contrary to his premises about Conchubar's conduct, he responds, in a parody of scientific method Yeats is to repeat in *The Resurrection*, not by re-examining the premises but by extending them to absorb the inconsistencies. As the Hebrew of

The Resurrection accounts for the empty tomb by concluding that the Romans have stolen Christ's body, Fergus accounts for the dark-faced men by surmising that they are merchants, for the missing messenger by assuming that Conchubar will come himself, and for the message when it arrives by arguing that some rogue has bribed its deliverer "to embroil us with the King" (399).

His meeting with the Musicians foreshadows the conflict, dramatized in the action proper, between wisdom wrought of instinct and imagination and the dictates of reason and policy. Behind the play lies the same inquiry into the sources of human knowledge lying behind *On Baile's Strand*; and Yeats suggests it, though mutedly, through the same ironic manipulation of labels. Observing Naoise duped into urging flight by Deirdre's threat of perfidy, Fergus calls him "Fool" (341). Diverting Fergus provoked by the messenger from his plan to confront Conchubar, Deirdre defines the true folly: "No, no, old man./ You thought the best, and the worst came of it;/ We listened to the counsel of the wise,/ And so turned fools" (402–405).

By insisting first that they trust Conchubar, then that they die at chess, like Lugaidh Redstripe and his lady, Naoise poses Deirdre with a variation on this dilemma. "Myself wars on myself," she confesses to the Musicians, "for I myself—/ That do my husband's will, yet fear to do it—/ Grow dragonish to myself" (163–65). Her image projects the feeling that, bejewelling her head and neck to greet the king instead of obeying her impulse to flee, she is maiming herself, and looks forward to her threat to maim herself indeed: "I'll spoil this beauty that brought misery/ And houseless wandering on the man I loved./ These wanderers will show me how to do it;/ To clip this hair to baldness, blacken my skin/ With walnut juice, and tear my face with briars" (360–64). It even more exactly prefigures the charms Conchubar has obtained to seduce Deirdre: those "strange, miracle-working, wicked stones" torn from "the heart and the hot brain/ Of Lybian dragons" and embroidered into the curtains of the marriage bed (267–69, 273–74).

Naoise admonishes Deirdre wishing her beauty spoiled to "Leave the gods' handiwork unblotched, and wait/ For their decision" (370–71). While he is acquiescing in the fate to which they are predestined, he is also urging her against violating nature. Violating nature is what Conchubar intends in preparing magical means to force the transfer of Deirdre's passion from her young husband to his aging self. It is, ironically, what Naoise effects in asking Deirdre to give over her passion and play the seamew. Her failure in the role delimits human potential, implying the difficulty inherent in their quest for "a high and comely end" (439):

> *Deirdre*. I cannot go on playing like that woman
>   That had but the cold blood of the sea in her veins.
> *Naoise*. It is your move. Take up your man again.
> *Deirdre*. Do you remember that first night in the woods
>   We lay all night on leaves, and looking up,
>   When the first grey of the dawn awoke the birds,
>   Saw leaves above us? You thought that I still slept,
>   And bending down to kiss me on the eyes,
>   Found they were open. Bend and kiss me now,
>   For it may be the last before our death.
>   And when that's over, we'll be different;
>   Imperishable things, a cloud or a fire.
>   And I know nothing but this body, nothing
>   But that old vehement, bewildering kiss.
>
> (486–99)

Deirdre pleads for life against Naoise, whom Yeats compares in his stage-directions to *"a man who has passed beyond life."* He aspires to the state of an image, a myth like Lugaidh Redstripe.

That the artist in Yeats sympathizes with Naoise's aspiration his work from *The Wanderings of Oisin* to *The Death of Cuchulain* recurrently shows. Years after *Deirdre*, he was to fashion in "Sailing to Byzantium" an extraordinary vehicle for capturing his own dream of passing beyond life: "Once out of nature I shall never take/ My bodily form from any natural thing" (25–26). But Yeats understands that discarding natural things as models for bodily form is impossible in nature; and so does Deirdre, who, looking forward to the imperishability she and Naoise may reach through death ("such a form as Grecian goldsmiths make" [27]), nonetheless recognizes that until then she must remain the passionate being she is.

Naoise discovers, at the appearance of Conchubar, that he too is incapable of keeping a marble or bronze repose. Overcome by the heroic passion of the embattled warrior, as Deirdre by the sexual passion of the beautiful woman, he rushes out to fight his antagonist. The whole scene, from the entrance of Naoise and Deirdre to Naoise's entanglement in Conchubar's net, turns on this moment, which upsets the young man's idealized view of himself as shaper of his own myth and of the king as repositor of a noble code. He greets Conchubar's coming with joy (*"laughing,"* the stage-directions specify) because it seems to him to affirm the ethos on which he orders his existence. Having joined Fergus in refusing to attach ominous intent to the lack of a messenger because "Being High King, [Conchubar] cannot break his faith" (169), having rejected Deirdre's proposal that they cut their way out because "I would have you die as a queen should" (424), he rises to Conchubar's apparent challenge exulting that, despite his broken faith, "there is kingly stuff in him" (503).

Naoise's disillusionment is measured by the change in his rhetoric. Apprised by the First Musician of Conchubar's actual design, "to spy upon you, not to fight" (504), he answers, "A prudent hunter, therefore, but no king./ He'd find if what has fallen in the pit/ Were worth the hunting, but has come too near,/ And I turn hunter. You're not man, but beast./ Go scurry in the bushes, now, beast, beast,/ For now it's topsy-turvy, I upon you" (505–10). He sees in Conchubar's stratagem the same corrupt, bourgeois motives impelling the king to bind Cuchulain with an oath; and shifting his attention from the Musicians to shout abuse after the departed monarch, he relinquishes the example of Lugaidh Redstripe to act his outraged self, as Deirdre acts herself in kneeling at his feet to beg a last kiss. The consequences of acting oneself, for both hero and heroine, are implicit in the animal imagery punctuating Naoise's anger. Reducing Conchubar to the status of beast, he is similarly reduced—if not to the bestial, to the merely human: a

hunter vengefully tracking his prey, and his world is reduced as
well from the heroic Ulster of ancient myth, in which men lived
by shared values, to the Darwinian jungle of modernity, bereft
of all values but survival of the fittest.

Naoise's rhetoric is to merge into reality as he returns,
"taken like a bird or a fish" (543). This transmutation of image
into action constitutes a significant advance in Yeats's progress
towards methods of staging the deeps of the mind.[5] He had used
it to advantage in the leprous moon of *The King's Threshold*,
which begins as a metaphor in Seanchan's mind and evolves
into a hand suspended in ironic blessing in the evening sky. But
the decay symbolized by the moon of *The King's Threshold* is in
process, and within the power of the imagination to reverse,
while in *Deirdre* the decay is complete: affirmed first by the
hegemony of a Conchubar no longer loyal to Ulster's noble
code, then by Naoise hunting the king as a beast, and finally by
Deirdre snatching the First Musician's knife. She realizes that
for herself and Naoise, as for Cuchulain caught between his
oath and his son, no viable alternative remains.

This scene, in its portrayal of Naoise's illusions gradually
pared away, is plotted to trace the growth of that realization. A
paradigm of their dilemma—defined spatially by their presence
in the king's guesthouse, temporally by the abased period in
which they live—Naoise's entrapment is presaged in the language he and Deirdre use. Supporting Fergus' disregard of both
Deirdre and the Musicians, he insists that he "will not weigh
the gossip of the roads/ With the King's word," and begs pardon
for his wife because "She has the heart of the wild birds that
fear/ The net of the fowler or the wicker cage" (300–303); to
which Deirdre replies, almost prophetically, by accepting his
characterization of her: "Am I to see the fowler and the cage/
And speak no word at all?" (304–305). Discovering their encir-
clement by Conchubar's men, Naoise (perhaps unconsciously)
acquiesces in her insight, reverting to the same mode of imagery: "The crib has fallen and the birds are in it" (418). Wit-

---

[5] Moore, *Masks of Love and Death*, p. 144, argues that it could almost be
said that in *Deirdre* "action becomes image and imagery action."

nessing her futile effort to soften the king's murderous resolve, he concedes, in still another permutation on the bird figure, their doom as, however noble, yet all too mortal quarry: "O my eagle!/ Why do you beat vain wings upon the rock/ When hollow night's above?" (606–608).

Naoise's enlightenment unfolds, then, through a series of changes wrought on a central image, in which sense the scene detailing its emergence anticipates a device Yeats supposedly gleaned from *Noh* and establishes itself as a metaphor of mind. His hero learns not merely that Conchubar has betrayed them but that the Musicians' way of apprehending truth is superior to Fergus': imagery becomes a more accurate index to truth than evidence.

The First Musician thus appropriates Naoise's image as, at the end, she and her colleagues start the process of embedding the lovers in myth: "Eagles have gone to their cloudy bed" (738). That the epitaph she pronounces over them comprises something larger than choric comment is suggested by the Musicians' shift from blank to rhymed verse, to a mode approaching the prosodic intricacy of their song on Edain. The First Musician's assertion answers the Second Musician's question, "What more is to be said?" (737). The dramatic rhythm informing their exchange repeats in miniature the rhythm of the play's opening scene, where the First Musician's announcement of her story provokes the Second Musician's comment, leading to the First Musician's venture into supplying the finish her tale lacks—"Hush! I have more to tell" (26)—which in turn blends into the action itself. Question and answer in the Musician's little dirge close a stichomythic sequence depicting them weaving about Deirdre and Naoise a formal lament, in the manipulation of their couplets, the repetition of phrase, the fabric of artifice:

> *First Musician.* They are gone, they are gone. The proud
>   may lie by the proud.
> *Second Musician.* Though we were bidden to sing, cry
>   nothing loud.
> *First Musician.* They are gone, they are gone.

Second Musician. Whispering were enough.
First Musician. Into the secret wilderness of their love.

$$(733-36)$$

The view inherent in their collaboration—that the truth of experience resides not in the facts but in the myth arising from it—partly manifests Yeats's interest in Nietzsche, to whom John Quinn introduced him in 1902.[6] Nietzsche had in *The Birth of Tragedy* cited with approval Schiller's understanding of the chorus as "the decisive step by which any naturalism in art was openly challenged."[7] And though *The Birth of Tragedy* appeared in English only in 1909, Yeats could have gleaned this pronouncement from Arthur Symons, whose review of Henri Albert's French translation of *The Birth of Tragedy*, published in *The Academy* for August 30, 1902, endeavors to summarize Nietzsche's theory. "In the admirable phrase of Schiller," writes Symons, paraphrasing Nietzsche, "the chorus is 'a living rampart against reality,' against that false reality of daily life which is a mere drapery of civilization, and which has nothing to do with the primitive reality of nature."[8] Yeats reinforces the function of his chorus as a rampart against the false reality of daily life, as an expression of myth's primacy over fact, by having even Fergus finally acknowledge this primacy. Faced with the dead lovers and a distraught Conchubar, he adopts Naoise's rhetoric: "What's this but empty cage and tangled wire/ Now the bird's gone?" (750–51). Words are, again, being recalled to their ancient sovereignty.

Deirdre stands as a commentary on its own value. The power of words is vested finally in the artist; and the Musicians are the artist's surrogates in the play. Commanded by Fergus to sing of the inconsequential, "a bubble" (117), or keep silent, they out-

[6] Alex Zwerdling, *Yeats and the Heroic Ideal* (New York: New York University Press, 1965), p. 20.

[7] *The Birth of Tragedy* and *The Genealogy of Morals*, trans. Francis Golffing (Garden City, New York: Doubleday, 1956), p. 20.

[8] See Symons, "Nietzsche on Tragedy," reprinted in *Plays, Acting, and Music* (New York: E.P. Dutton, 1909), p. 13. For a history of the English reception of Nietzsche, see David S. Thatcher, *Nietzsche in England 1890–1914* (Toronto: The University of Toronto Press, 1970).

wit him by evoking Edain, whose story also entails rivalry in love, death, and a game of chess. The stanza in which all three Musicians join makes their intent plain:

> But is Edain worth a song
>   Now the hunt begins anew?
> Praise the beautiful and strong;
>   Praise the redness of the yew;
> Praise the blossoming apple-stem.
>   But our silence had been wise.
> What is all our praise to them
>   That have one another's eyes?

(141–48)

These lines seem to celebrate not Edain choosing Eochaid and, as Yeats has her put it in *The Two Kings*, a "nest upon a narrow ledge/ Above a windy precipice" (194–95) over Midir and immortality but Deirdre and Naoise united against the malevolence of Conchubar. The hunt begins anew for them; and the First Musician brings this motif, crucial to the figurative substructure of the play, to logical completion in her portrayal of the lovers dead, sequestered in the wilderness of their love. Deirdre herself becomes metaphorically the blossoming apple-stem which, matured to fruitfulness, Conchubar "had [in his own words] to climb the topmost bough, and pull/ . . . among the winds" (744–45).

Song is rendered an instrument of prophecy. Through the constellation of Edain and her "goodman," Lugaidh Redstripe and his lady, Deirdre and Naoise, the mythic past foreshadows the immediate future. Myth blends into history. For the tale of Lugaidh Redstripe is, as the chess set on the table indicates, represented as history; and so is the tale of Deirdre and Naoise.

Conflating myth and history is an artistic prerogative Yeats examines in *Discoveries* (1906), observing of "fine literature" that there is in it "something of an old wives' tale":

> The makers of it are like an old peasant telling stories of the great famine or the hangings of '98 or from his memories. He

has felt something in the depth of his mind and he wants to make it as visible and powerful to our senses as possible.[9]

These observations are gathered under the head, "Has the Drama of Contemporary Life a Root of Its Own?" Yeats is renewing from still another platform his attack on Ibsenite realism, what he calls with deliberate dreariness, also in *Discoveries*, "The Play of Modern Manners."[10] He is not, however, denying art a relation to perceived reality—his peasant's stories arise from circumstances, historical or personal. He is arguing instead that circumstances alone are just that—circumstantial; that they acquire significance by being fashioned into symbols of psychic reality, conveying visibly and powerfully something felt in the depth of the mind. As he had asked in "The Play, the Player, and the Scene," "is not the greatest play not the play that gives the sensation of external reality but the play in which there is the greatest abundance of life itself, of the reality that is in our mind?"[11]

By this definition, fine literature in general and great drama in particular consist of psychic metaphors. The Musicians in *Deirdre* are old wives, getting the story right for preservation and transmission to the descendants of ancient Ireland. That they recognize in the fate of its protagonists a pattern comparable to those informing the stories of Edain and Lugaidh Redstripe attests to its archetypal character. It is imprinted on the psyche of the race.

Translating racial archetypes into discrete dramatic entities constitutes, for Yeats, the peculiar virtue of art. "Literature," he argues, in an untitled piece from *Samhain* for 1904, "is not journalism because it can turn the imagination to whatever is essential and unchanging in life."[12] The use of a chorus as a way of emphasizing how *Deirdre* embraces the essential and unchanging in life once more reflects Yeats's communion with Nietzsche, who described the satyric chorus behind Greek tragedy as "nature beings who dwell behind all civilization and

[9] *Essays and Introductions*, p. 276.   [10] *Ibid.*, p. 274.
[11] *Explorations*, p. 167.   [12] *Ibid.*, p. 140.

preserve their identity through every change of generations and historical movement."[13] They express a wisdom beyond time and place; and Yeats incorporates this wisdom in his Musicians, who, through their fund of mythic knowledge, transcend time and, as nomads, are without place: "We have no country," the First Musician tells Fergus, "but the roads of the world" (52).

Having no country, they belong to all countries. In their homelessness they are akin to Deirdre, who also conceives of herself as having no country but the roads of the world. The First Musician addresses her colleagues as "my wanderers" (1). Deirdre pleading with Naoise asks, "Were we not born to wander?" (342). In a speech he was later to cancel Yeats has even Fergus at least unconsciously discern this kinship, referring to the Musicians as "Birds out of the waste" (157).

Birds out of the waste comprise the image by which Deirdre and Naoise depict themselves. And Deirdre makes their birdness the rhetorical climax of her argument to Naoise for the virtue of wandering: "These jewels have been reaped by the innocent sword/ Upon a mountain, and a mountain bred me ;/ But who can tell what change can come to love/ Among the Valleys? I speak no falsehood now./ Away to windy summits, and there mock/ The night-jar and the valley-keeping birds!" (343–48).

Her appeal prefigures their metaphorical ascent as eagles, and through its imagery of height defines the solitude which is their lot. In this imagery too her rhetoric and that of the Musicians singing of Edain converge. Their song manifests an early instance of what was to become the identifying Yeatsian symbol of isolation:

> 'Why is it', Queen Edain said,
>   'If I do but climb the stair
> To the tower overhead,
>   When the winds are calling there,
> Or the Gannets calling out
>   In waste places of the sky,
> There's so much to think about
>   That I cry, that I cry?'

                                                            (125–32)

[13] *The Birth of Tragedy*, p. 50.

Conjoining the tower, the calling wind, and waste places, by analogy those from which the Musicians (birdlike) are said to come, Edain's question implies a bond among isolation, love's emotional overflow, and creative experience. The Musicians are themselves lovers. When Deirdre asks their leader if she has been in love, she answers: "There is nothing in the world/ That has been friendly to us but the kisses/ That were upon our lips, and when we are old/ Their memory will be all the life we have" (231–34). In their song she and the Second Musician take roles, one as Edain, the other as Eochaid—from the perspective of the audience visually blending the states of singer and lover.

This blending is what the antiphonal structure of the song is meant to stress. To Edain's question, Eochaid replies:

> 'Love would be a thing of naught
> Had not all his limbs a stir
>   Born out of immoderate thought;
> Were he anything by half,
>   Were his measure running dry.
> Lovers, if they may not laugh,
>   Have to cry, have to cry.'
>
>   (134–40)

The second stanza glosses the first; and in its proposal that love exists only by total immersion of the self the song as a whole glosses the choice Deirdre and Naoise make. Putting this proposal in the mouth of one of the Musicians suggests again Yeats's debt to Nietzsche. Defining love as a kind of abandon labels it an outgrowth of the Dionysiac in man. In his paraphrase of *The Birth of Tragedy* Symons aligns himself with Nietzsche's discovery of the germ of the chorus in hymns to Dionysus, characterizing it as "the 'lyric cry,' the vital ecstasy."[14] And Nietzsche himself finds in folk song "the classical instance of a union between Apollonian and Dionysiac intentions."[15] By which he means that folk song generates from a people's orgiastic tendencies, given order through the controlling genius of a singer.

Travelling minstrels, the Musicians are repositors of the folk

[14] *Plays, Acting, and Music*, p. 13.   [15] *The Birth of Tragedy*, p. 42.

tradition. Continually present yet marginally participant, they embody the consciousness absorbing Deirdre and Naoise into that tradition, imposing the order of song on the turbulence wrought by human passion. They function comparably to Nietzsche's idea of the Greek chorus, which he termed "the 'ideal spectator' inasmuch as it is the only *seer*—seer of the visionary world of the proscenium."[16]

Yeats's wish to render the Musicians the "ideal spectator" of his world is mirrored in the passivity he has them bespeak as their proper stance. When Deirdre reads in the First Musician's analogy of Conchubar's love to the love of an old miser for the dragon-stone a warning that he will kill Naoise and claim her for himself, the Musician responds: " 'Tis you that put that meaning upon words/ Spoken at random" (256–57). When Deirdre wrests the knife from the First Musician, she comments: "You have taken it,/ I did not give it you." (516–17).

The Musicians, then, help to move the action, yet seek to remove themselves from it. They are of the world of the play, yet distanced from it. In the duality of their perspective they adumbrate the Musicians of the dance plays, who hover at the edges of the action both to set its scene and, through their songs, to establish the symbolic framework by which it accrues larger significance. Though Yeats has still to hone this technique into the extraordinarily refined instrument it is to become in *At the Hawk's Well*, he is in the pivotal scene of Deirdre and Naoise at chess shaping the Musicians to the same end. They announce Conchubar's arrival as their counterparts in *At the Hawk's Well* announce the arrivals of the Old Man and the Young Man. They verbalize the king's motives as the Musicians in *At the Hawk's Well* verbalize the motives of the Old Man and the Young Man. They spin out the symbolic dimension of the scene through song:

> Love is an immoderate thing
>> And can never be content
> Till it dip an ageing wing
>> Where some laughing element

---

[16] *Ibid.*, p. 54.

Leaps and Time's old lanthorn dims.
  What's the merit in love-play,
In the tumult of the limbs
  That dies out before 'tis day,
Heart on heart, or mouth on mouth,
  All that mingling of our breath,
When love-longing is but drouth
  For the things come after death?

(474–85)

While Yeats's stage-directions indicate no necessary link between this song and the song of Edain, his prosody all but insists on the one as coda to the other. Both proceed by four-
stress, alternately rhymed lines, tending toward strong accents
on the opening syllable. Though the song of Edain falls into oc-
taves while the song accompanying the chess game is of a single
twelve-line piece, the language in the second echoes the language in the first. The "immoderate thing" love is described as
being in the coda recalls the "immoderate thought" said to stir
love's limbs in the verses on Edain. The difference is between an
evocation of something past—existing for the Musicians as
thought, the stuff of images held in the mind's eye—and an
elaboration on the thing happening. The lyrical backdrop to the
chess game unfolds as life. Its audience is witness to the reciprocity between image and action, myth and history.

Yeats emphasizes this reciprocity through two features of
Deirdre to figure increasingly in his later *Noh*-oriented Cuchulain plays, its brevity and the foreknowledge of its audience.
The proximity of the songs allows the audience to hold the details simultaneously in memory. The familiarity of the story allows them to construe their symbolic meaning and respond to
their prophetic resonances, thus preparing them not only for
the tragic climax but for the new song the Musicians are com-
posing even as the lovers go to their cloudy bed. Portraying love
as a bird doomed to dip an aging wing renders the song sung to
the chess game Januslike: it looks back through the bird images
lacing the speeches of Deirdre and Naoise to the Musicians'
guarded depiction of them as hunted quarry and forward to
their apotheosis as eagles. Woven into the sequence at the

play's dramatic center, it crystallizes the pattern giving *Deirdre*
rhetorical unity.

In posing the question, of what merit is sexual ecstasy which
actually expresses a longing for things after death, it also re-
phrases from the obverse angle the question posed in the song
of Edain: what can the Musicians' praise be to those "That have
one another's eyes?" Implicit in both questions is a tragic view
of life Yeats gleaned perhaps partly from Nietzsche, who
epitomized Dionysiac wisdom in Silenus' reply to the demand
of King Midas that he reveal man's greatest good: "Ephemeral
wretch, begotten by accident and toil, why do you force me to
tell you what it would be your greatest boon not to hear? What
would be best for you is quite beyond your reach: not to have
been born, not to *be*, to be *nothing*. But the second best is to die
soon."[17] The intimacy Nietzsche detected between Dionysiac
passion and the wish for death underlies Yeats's lyric treatment
of desire as a yearning for things after death, and accounts for
the mythic thrust toward death not only of *Deirdre* but of *On
Baile's Strand*, and it may be of the Cuchulain saga in general.

For Nietzsche, however, death made an end: its virtue was its
promise of nothingness. Whereas Yeats, as the song's last line
establishes, projects his dramatic cosmos beyond death.
Nietzsche, tracing the course of Greek culture, argued that by
fabricating a pantheon of Olympians, for whom human pleas-
ures were integral to divine life, the adherents of Apollo reversed the Dionysiac orientation: "it became possible to stand
the wisdom of Silenus on its head and proclaim that it was the
worst evil for men to die soon, and second worst for him to die
at all."[18] Yeats, writing to John Quinn in May, 1903, professes
a leaning toward Apollo: "I have always felt that the soul has
two movements primarily: one to transcend forms, and the
other to create forms. Nietzsche . . . calls these the Dionysiac
and the Apollonic respectively. I think I have to some extent got
weary of that wild god Dionysus, and I am hoping that the
Far-Darter will come in his place."[19]

The Far-Darter materializes in the play through the Musi-

[17] *Ibid.*, p. 29.   [18] *Ibid.*, p. 30.
[19] Wade, *Letters*, p. 403.

cians, not only because they impose form on experience but because they show by their art a way to life beyond death, which
is what Deirdre acknowledges about them in giving their leader
her bracelet as token that they have the story right. The question closing the Musicians' second song responds to the question closing their first. Though their accession to Deirdre's
request for silence seems to concede that the praise of the
Musicians is nothing to lovers, their claim—borne out by
events—that love is truly consummated alone through death
suggests that the praise of the Musicians is everything. In it lies
immortality.

Its power to grant immortality is asserted by Deirdre herself
as, rejecting the First Musician's advice that she use her
"woman's wile" (525) to placate Conchubar, as she prepares to
confer her bracelet: "Women, if I die,/ If Naoise die this night,
how will you praise?/ What words seek out? for that will stand
to you;/ For being but dead we shall have many friends" (528–
31). Her expectation that, through death, they will gain friends
recalls her plea to Naoise to "go out and fight"/ because "Our
way of life has brought no friends to us,/ And if we do not buy
them leaving it,/ We shall be ever friendless" (429–32). Her
conviction that friendship, for them, will be measured by the
imprint they leave on the consciousness of the race is Naoise's
conviction too. It is in answer to her plea that he proposes
Lugaidh Redstripe as their model.

The friends of Deirdre and Naoise are ultimately the audience
at Yeats's play. By having his protagonists plot their conduct as
a quest for such friends, he draws the audience into his dramatic
construct. They culminate the process that is the scenario; their
presence attests to the triumph inherent in the tragedy.

Drawing the audience into *Deirdre* reflects one of Yeats's
early efforts at breaking those dykes between man and man,
which very few years later he was to announce as his ideal for
the tragic theater; at achieving the communality he would seek
again by reducing his audience to "forty or fifty readers of
poetry," discarding western dramatic conventions, and aban-
doning the Abbey for Lady Cunard's sitting-room. Describing
the performance of *At the Hawk's Well* hosted by Lady

Cunard, Yeats observes of Ito's dance that "One realized anew, at every separating strangeness, that the measure of all arts' greatness can be but in their intimacy."[20] His assumption that separating strangenesses contribute to art's intimacy also affects *Deirdre*, the scenario of which traces the progressive separation of its heroine, and then of its hero, from the ethos of Fergus and Conchubar.

The play's focus narrows as the situation evolves. In its first half impetus is supplied by Fergus: he guides the lovers, arranges the Musicians' welcome, and shapes the attitude Naoise adopts toward the threat Deirdre and the Musicians perceive. The second half belongs to Deirdre, consisting wholly in her struggle to find a manner—I would almost say a mask—which will enable her to control her fate.

This shift begins with the entrance of the messenger, set midway into the scenario. His message crystallizes Deirdre's need to choose between death with her lover and life with his murderer, between Dionysus and Apollo: the wisdom of Silenus that the greatest good man can hope is to die soon and its Apollonic inversion that dying soon is the worst of evils. Her conduct is throughout a struggle, given over only when Naoise is killed, to avoid accepting the necessity of death.

The futility of the struggle—Yeats's dramatic insistence that the hero must, however reluctantly, choose Dionysus—is conveyed not alone by the audience's awareness of how Deirdre's tale ends but by her scheme for coping with her crisis. She creates roles, if you will masks, tried on one after another, each proving antagonistic ("dragonish") to her true self and failing, until at last she finds a role promising her room in that narrow bride-bed where she and her man will "lie close up . . . and . . . outsleep the cock-crow" (731–32).[21]

Deirdre involves, that is, the rudiments of a play within the

---

[20] "Certain Noble Plays of Japan," p. 241.

[21] Peter Ure, *Yeats the Playwright* (New York: Barnes & Noble, 1963), p. 53, characterizes the second half of *Deirdre* as the heroine's attempt to change the story from inside it by assuming roles. And Moore, *Masks of Love and Death*, p. 142, judges Deirdre herself psychologically the most complex of Yeats's heroines "because her struggle to *be* a heroine is the essential action of the play."

play, thereby anticipating a Yeatsian strategy to emerge fullblown in major innovative efforts like *The Only Jealousy of Emer*, *The Player Queen*, *The Words Upon the Window-Pane*, and *Purgatory*. While the play within the play becomes the substance of the action as action becomes more and more a mirror of Deirdre's mind, it infuses the part of the scenario energized primarily by Fergus too: unwinding from Deirdre's use of the Musicians'raddle to prepare a face (don a mask) for meeting Conchubar to her attempt to dupe Naoise into flight by feigning interest in Conchubar.

Its gradual envelopment of the scenario as a whole reflects the rising conflict in her between desire for life and the demands of myth. Yeats builds his drama, as Clark stresses, toward recognition;[22] and the recognition on which *Deirdre* focuses is chiefly its heroine's own. At the turning-point, when Conchubar's design is exposed, Yeats consequently removes his other principals from the stage, Fergus to rouse his people, Naoise to hunt the king, permitting them to return either, as in Fergus's case, too late to act or, as in Naoise's, made helpless to act.

What the audience sees, then—who appears in the scene, how the scene is blocked—Yeats renders a medium of symbolic communication. Grouping Deirdre with the Musicians around the brazier on one side of the stage, Naoise and Fergus at the chess board on its opposite side adumbrates, as Clark again argues, the dynamics of the tragedy.[23] When Fergus *"brings"* Naoise to the table, he is asserting his control over events, his faith that human passions submit to the same rational ordering as a game of chess. When Deirdre gravitates to the Musicians, she is acknowledging her kinship with them as free agents, natural beings governed neither by law nor noble code but by instinct and imagination. When the Musicians kindle the torches from their brazier, they are identifying instinct and imagination as vehicles of enlightenment for their world.[24]

Yeats is using stage imagery as he might use imagery brought to the mind's eye by words in a poem. In the song sung

---

[22] *Yeats and the Theatre of Desolate Reality*, especially pp. 26 and 30.

[23] *Ibid.*, pp. 34–36.

[24] *Ibid.*, p. 34.

to the chess game love is portrayed as finding contentment only where "Time's old Lanthorn dims." And Time's old lanthorn is dimming even as the First Musician announces her story. Yeats's stage-directions call for a *"sky dimming, night closing in."* While the song seems to lament the decay of passion through age, Naoise and Deirdre anticipate its relevance to them, couching their request that the Musicians accompany their game in language prefiguring its lyrics. Deirdre appeals to them to praise herself and Naoise for their love, "And praise the double sunset, for naught's lacking/ But a good end to the long, cloudy day" (466–67). Naoise commands them to "Light torches there and drive the shadows out,/ For the day's grey end comes up" (468–69). At the play's end, when Conchubar orders the curtain opened, disclosing the tragedy in all its dimensions, his house *"is lit in the glare of . . . torches."*

These torches are held by retainers of Fergus. Spectators at the scene, they stand to it as the audience, for whom—the shadows driven out—the mythic pattern is revealed in its completeness. Deirdre's stratagems are understood as her quest, triggered by her discovery that she cannot be the sea mew, to find a heroic identity of her own. Turning the play into a near monologue, in which Deirdre shapes her own myth, Yeats appears to have adapted to his purposes a device Synge had employed in *Riders to the Sea* (1904), where Maurya, after the drowning of Bartley, takes over to keen, also in a near monologue, the loss of her husband, her husband's father, and her six sons.

Yeats's scenario does not, however, close as Synge's does, fixed on his heroine at her most intense tragic moment. If Yeats structuring his final scene profited by the dramatic genius of his friend and Abbey co-director, what he borrowed would seem to have come from *Playboy of the Western World* (1907), which Synge was gestating during the time Yeats was writing *Deirdre* (suggesting that the debt may have run in reverse). For the last act of *Playboy* proceeds through a dazzling sequence of false endings, parodying the comic conventions from which it departs and hinting to the audience that Christy need not have fared as well as he did.

While Yeats exploits this technique in a much more re-strained way, and to very different effect, *Deirdre* too presents the audience with an ending which is not the end. Refusing to believe that his chosen queen has escaped him by joining her husband in death, challenged by Fergus' defiance of his author-ity (I'll not have you touch it" [751]), Conchubar turns on his tormentors in rage and self-pity: "You are all traitors, all against me—all./ And she has deceived me for a second time;/ And every common man can keep his wife,/ But not the King" (752–55). At which point, presumably, the curtain descends and the audience leaves satisfied. Conchubar has shown himself unworthy of Deirdre, as we knew he would. The lovers have died for their love, showing themselves worthy of tragic stat-ure, as we knew they would. Fergus is left, like Horatio in *Hamlet*, a sadder yet wiser man, to clean up the mess and re-store a semblance of order. All the moral and metaphysical sub-tleties of the play have been neatly sorted out.

But the curtain does not descend. The shouts of "Death to Conchubar!" "Where is Naoise?" seem instead to open a new line of action, in which, faced with the threat of revolt, Con-chubar emerges a heroic figure:

> [. . . *The dark-faced men gather round Conchubar and draw their swords; but he motions them away.*]
>   I have no need of weapons,
> There's not a traitor that dare stop my way.
> Howl, if you will; but I, being King, did right
> In choosing her most fitting to be Queen,
> And letting no boy lover take the sway.
>
>   (755–59)

Making this gesture and its attendant claim the real culmination of the play not only gives Conchubar the last word but im-presses on us a portrait of him as possessed of power and cour-age. It contradicts the contempt Naoise evinces, and we share, in pursuing the king as a beast.

Yeats sends his audience home forced to rethink their as-sumptions about Conchubar's villainy, because he would not have Conchubar dismissed as a mere villain. Sketching in the backdrop to her story, the First Musician accounts for the king's love of Deirdre, observing that "She put on womanhood, and he lost peace" (19). Calling attention to the arrival of the messenger, Fergus cries, "Peace, peace" (372). And underlying the tragedy is Conchubar's struggle to find peace. Love is no less "immoderate" for him than for Deirdre and Naoise. He too is gripped by a Dionysiac passion, which he must follow out to its inevitable extreme. If the thrust of the action is to dramatize his betrayal not only of the lovers but of their guarantor, of the heroic world and its values, he reminds us at the end that he too has been betrayed.

Insofar, indeed, as the audience is expected to bring to the theater an acquaintance with the tale as traditionally told, and especially the dire prophecy overhanging Deirdre's birth, all the actors in this tragedy appear victims of a grim cosmic joke. They are, as Yeats's dialogue repeatedly insists, mocked. When Deirdre professes to have put on beauty for Conchubar, Naoise accuses her of "mocking" him (328). When she urges flight—itself, as she sees, a mocking gesture—Fergus warns that "King Conchubar may think that he is mocked/ and the house blaze again" (352–53). When Naoise pursues the messenger, intending to challenge Conchubar before his court, "The Lybian, knowing that a servant's life/ Is safe from hands like mine, but turned and mocked" (412–13). When he pursues Conchubar himself, to the cry of "beast, beast," he is also mocking. And when he comes back netted, to hear the king offer leniency, he understands that Conchubar "is but mocking us" (551).

His understanding parallels Conchubar's own of Deirdre's comparable attempt at prevarication. To her request that she be allowed to perform the customary duties of a wife toward her dead husband, Conchubar replies, "You are deceiving me" (689). His accusation echoes syntactically Naoise's accusation of Deirdre feigning interest in Conchubar, that she is mocking him, as Naoise's epithet for the king, "Beast, beast," echoes and mocks Fergus's announcement of the messenger. Deception and mockery are of a piece. And it is one aspect of the complex irony Yeats achieves in *Deirdre* that Conchubar, at least half-knowingly, permits himself to be deceived. He too comprehends himself engaged in a mythic action from which there is no escape; he too accepts, in his way, responsibility for preserving traditional values. That Yeats discerns in this situation, even as it unfolds tragically, the potential for mocking man's enterprise reflects his grasp of how thin a line divides tragedy from farce. The thinness of this line he is to explore in the very next of his Cuchulain plays, *The Green Helmet*, in which once more the protagonist sets his life against the abasement of the ancient world, but in which too his grand gesture is treated as part of what its poet calls "An Heroic Farce."

IV

"I Choose the Laughing Lip"

"I have," Yeats announces in *Discoveries*, "always come to this certainty: what moves natural men in the arts is what moves them in life, and that is, intensity of personal life, intonations that show them, in a book or a play, the strength, the essential moment of a man who would be exciting in the market or at the dispensary door. They most go out of the theatre with the strength that they live by strengthened from looking upon some passion that could, whatever its chosen way of life, strike down an enemy, fill a long stocking with money or move a girl's heart."[1] From remarks on "Personality and the Intellectual Essences," this statement suggests the kind of dramatic orientation by which Yeats sought to drown the dykes separating himself from his audience, and recalls his famous argument for the likeness of farce and tragedy. The "essential moment" of the man on the Yeatsian stage is the "moment of intense life" comprising the action of farce or tragedy. The passion on which the audience looks—and which the man becomes—is rendered through the insulation of its moment from all other moments, its projection as "an energy, an eddy of life purified from everything but itself."

Yeats's way of purifying this eddy in *The Green Helmet* is manifest in the reduction of his source, specified in his Notes as *"The Feast of Bricriu . . .* in *Cuchulain of Muirthemne,"* to one episode.[2] As Birgit Bjersby pointed out long ago, he combines Bricriu, who provokes the quarrel among Laegaire, Conall, and Cuchulain over the Championship of Ulster, with Curoi, who

---

[1] *Essays and Introductions*, p. 265.

[2] See the *Variorum Plays*, p. 454. While Yeats singles out "Bricriu's Feast" as providing the substance of his plot, in fact the story, as Skene, *Cuchulain Plays*, p. 27, observes, extends through two chapters of *Cuchulain of Muirthemne*, the first called "Bricriu's Feast and the War of Words of the Women of Ulster," and the second, which provides the real dramatic focus for the play, "The Championship of Ulster."

resolves it.[3] He also eliminates the feast occasioning the quarrel and the War of Words among the contenders' wives, as well as the various trials preceding Curoi's challenge. Then, further refining his treatment of the tale from its initial (prose) version in *The Golden Helmet* (1908) to its final version as *The Green Helmet* two years later, he redraws Cuchulain's motive for laying his head on the Red Man's block, muting the hero's claim to be sacrificing himself for the peace of the country, stressing the import of his sacrifice as an expression of the same noble ethos at stake in *Deirdre*.[4] To the Red Man's demand in *The Golden Helmet*, Cuchulain announces: "The quarrels of Ireland shall end. What is one man's life? I will pay the debt with my own head"; and when Emer starts to wail, he adds: "Do not cry out, Emer, for if I were not myself, if I were not Cuchulain, one of those that God has made reckless, the women of Ireland had not loved me, and you had not held your head so high." To the Red Man's demand in *The Green Helmet*, he replies: "He played and paid with his head, and it's right that we pay him back,/ And give him more than he gave, for he comes in here as a guest:/ So I will give him my head" (262–64); and when Emer begins her keen, he adds: "Little wife, little wife, be at rest./ Alive I have been far off in all lands under the sun,/ And been no faithful man; but when my story is done/ My fame shall spring up and laugh, and set you high above all" (264–67). The change reflects the economy and concreteness Yeats achieves in verse. The twin focuses of Cuchulain's speech in *The Golden Helmet*—one on his responsibility to Ireland, the other on his need to fulfill himself, both weighed equally through the interruption of Emer breaking the speech into distinct halves—are condensed in *The Green Helmet* into the imagery of game, gift, and guest. The shift in *The Green Helmet* version, again signaled by Emer, opens a new dimension to Cuchulain's consciousness and to the play.

[3] *The Interpretation of the Cuchulain Legend in the Works of W.B. Yeats* (Upsala: A.B. Lundequistska Bokhandeln, 1950), p. 33.

[4] See A.B. Bushrui, *Yeats's Verse-Plays: The Revisions 1900–1910* (Oxford: Clarendon Press, 1965), pp. 180–81 and 194, where the change in Cuchulain's motive is examined.

For Cuchulain, like Deirdre and Naoise, sees himself by his conduct as writing his own story, making myth of his own life. He rejects the domesticity of Laegaire and Conall, who stay at home relying on their wives to boast their strength, and (once more like Deirdre and Naoise) elects to wander. Indeed he adopts their mode of imagery, analogizing his choice for death, the ultimate wanderlust, to that of "the great barnacle-goose/ When its eyes are turned to the sea and its beak to the salt of the air" (270–71).

The image would have evoked for the Abbey audience Ireland's wild geese spreading their gray wings on the tides of her tragic history; and Cuchulain appears at the outset an exile unexpectedly returned. It is to emphasize the exile in Cuchulain, alien even among his own folk, that Yeats reverts to a device he employs over and over, and which Synge made one of his dramaturgic signatures, beginning the action with the hero off-stage. The curtain rises on Laegaire and Conall in postures of fear and alarm, accentuated by the refrain-like repetition of Laegaire's question, "Does anything stir on the sea?" and Conall's answer, "Not even a fish or a gull" (7 and 64), occurring first as Cuchulain's distant shout reaches them, then as they prepare to tell their tale. This refrain, the play's strong, sometimes intricate rhyme scheme, its anapestic fourteeners, intermittently divisible into lines alternating four and three stresses (which Yeats himself late in life was to describe as "ballad metre"), its sequences of incremental repetition are perhaps reasons why Moore properly labels *The Green Helmet* a dramatic ballad.[5]

Its dialogue, that is, seems geared toward narration. Yeats may have gleaned the tendency to allow characters speeches often amounting to narrative set pieces, more pronounced in the earlier prose version of the play, from Wilfrid Scawen Blunt's *Fand*, performed at the Abbey in 1907, and supposedly the germ of his desire to rework *The Golden Helmet* into rhymed verse.[6] The highly mannered, almost static acting a

[5] *Masks of Love and Death*, p. 155. For Yeats's description of the meter, see "A General Introduction for My Work," *Essays and Introductions*, p. 523.

[6] See Bushrui, *Yeats's Verse-Plays*, p. 184.

play like *Fand* must have required conforms to Yeats's demand that movement be subordinated to language, and in general to the view of drama he had been promoting since he had begun to think of writing for the theater. In 1902 he returned from a performance of Sarah Bernhardt and De Max in *Phedra*, proclaiming it "the most beautiful thing I had ever seen upon the stage":

> For long periods the performers would merely stand and pose, and I once counted twenty-seven quite slowly before anybody on a fairly well-filled stage moved, as it seemed, so much as an eyelash. The periods of stillness were generally shorter, but I frequently counted seventeen, eighteen, or twenty before there was a movement. I noticed, too, that the gestures had a rhythmic progression. Sarah Bernhardt would keep her hands clasped over, let us say, her right breast for some time, and then move them till she had exhausted all the gestures of uplifted hands. Through one long scene De Max, who was quite as fine, never lifted his hand above his elbow, and it was only when the emotion came to its climax that he raised it to his breast. Beyond them stood a crowd of white-robed men who never moved at all, and the whole scene had the nobility of Greek sculpture, and an extraordinary reality and intensity.[7]

For Yeats, the performance of Bernhardt and De Max became another blow struck in the battle against Ibsenite realism. It "made me understand, in a new way," he concludes of their *Phedra*, "that saying of Goethe's which is understood everywhere but in England, 'Art is art because it is not nature'."[8] The deliberately anti-naturalistic style Yeats discovered in the Bernhardt-De Max *Phedra*, and presumably in *Fand*, produced in lieu of action a series of static stage pictures effective perhaps for tragedy, at least of the kind Yeats was to write from his encounter with *Noh*, but inimical to farce. Even while recasting the essentially natural prose cadences of *The Golden Helmet* as the jog-trotting couplets of *The Green Helmet*, he

[7] From an essay in *Samhain*, 1902. *Explorations*, p. 87.
[8] *Ibid.*, p. 88.

was fragmenting the play's patches of uninterrupted discourse, giving his speakers discernible motives and their speeches dramatic immediacy. Conall's assurance to Laegaire that nothing stirs on the sea, and he "can see for a mile or two, now that the moon's at the full" (8) responds in *The Golden Helmet* not to Laegaire's anxious question but to Yeats's need for exposition. The opening speech of the play, it is too obviously uttered as much for the audience as for Conall's frightened cohort: "Not a sail, not a wave, and if the sea were not purring a little like a cat, not a sound. There is no danger yet. I can see a long way for the moonlight is on the sea."

Cuchulain too seems often in *The Golden Helmet* to be talking across the situation to the gallery. When he finds his presence menaced by Laegaire, both his defiance and the surprise of his companions on recognizing him are largely lost amid abstractions draining the moment of tension:

> *Leagerie [drawing his sword].* Go out of this, or I will make you. [*The Young Man seizes Leagerie's arm, and thrusting it up, passes him, and puts his shield over the chair, where there is an empty place.*]
>
> *Young Man [at table].* It is here I will spend the night, but I won't tell you why until I have drunk. I am thirsty. What, the flagon full and the cups empty and Leagerie and Conal there! Why, what's in the wind that Leagerie and Conal cannot drink?
>
> *Leagerie.* It is Cuchulain.[9]

In *The Green Helmet* their meeting is transformed:

> *Laegaire.* Go out or I will make you.
>
> *Young Man [forcing up Laegaire's arm, passing him and putting his shield on the wall over the chair].* Not till I have drunk my fill,
>
> But may some dog defend me, for a cat of wonder's up.

[9] I have taken the liberty of deleting the interpolations by which Alspach notes the changes from the first edition of *The Golden Helmet* to its reprinting in *Collected Works*, IV (both 1908). The changes cannot be read altogether intelligibly without the apparatus of the *Variorum* for reference; and they are too minor to make any real difference to the play.

Laegaire and Conall are here, the flagon full to the top,
And the cups—

Laegaire.	It is Cuchulain.
Cuchulain.	The cups are dry as a bone.

(43–46)

Cuchulain reacts by a metaphor not only consistent in its extravagance with the milieu the play calls for, which the stage-directions describe as *"violent and startling,"* but ironically resonant of the confrontation to form its crisis. As most of the Abbey audience, and any reader of *Cuchulain of Muirthemne*, would have known, Cuchulain is the Hound of Culain, the dog who defends Culain's house and, at the ford, all of Ulster rather than being defended. The cat of wonder, less vividly evoked in the purring sea of *The Golden Helmet*, prefigures the Red Man, his trophy ("this cat that has come to take our lives" [152]), and his feline attendants, against whom—inverting once more his own image—Cuchulain defends the honor of the land.

Yeats measures the odds on Laegaire and Conall sitting at a table with full flagon and empty cups, and Cuchulain's astonishment at so finding them, by putting a metaphor in his mouth that turns reality on its head. He also cuts away the dead verbiage muffling the intensity of the scene in *The Golden Helmet*. Cuchulain's insistence on staying the night and his profession of thirst, sprawled over three independent clauses of prose, compress into a half-line of poetry. His hint that he has special reasons for staying, to lead nowhere in the plotting of the play, disappears.

Moreover, Yeats alters the scene's rhythm, rhetorically and dramatically, giving Cuchulain's astonishment an impact barely felt in *The Golden Helmet*. The order of his perceptions is reversed—from the full flagon, the empty cups, Laegaire and Conall to Laegaire and Conall, the full flagon, and the empty cups—building to a comic climax, accentuated not only by transmuting a simple assertion, that the cups are empty, into an image with visual and tactile appeal, the cups dry as a bone, but also by isolating it through Laegaire's interruption.

Making Laegaire's acknowledgment of Cuchulain a sort of

parenthesis in the last line of Cuchulain's speech, thereby holding the speech in suspension like a periodic sentence,
exemplifies one of the features distinguishing *The Green Helmet* from its theatrically flaccid archetype, and anticipates
Yeats's solution to a major problem posed by his scenario: getting the Red Man's appearances recounted without undermining the drama as drama in the process. In *The Golden Helmet*
Yeats has Conall, as Laegaire actually urges him to do in *The
Green Helmet*, "tell it all out to the end" (60):

> Cuchulain, a little while after you went out of this country
> we were sitting here drinking. We were merry. It was late,
> close on to midnight, when a strange-looking man with red
> hair and a great sword in his hand came in through that door.
> He asked for ale and we gave it to him, for we were tired of
> drinking with one another. He became merry, and for every
> joke we made he made a better, and presently we all three got
> up and danced, and then we sang, and then he said he would
> show us a new game. He said he would stoop down and that
> one of us was to cut off his head, and afterwards one of us, or
> whoever has ["had" in the second printing] a mind for the
> game, was to stoop down and have his head whipped off.
> 'You take off my head,' said he, 'and then I take off his head,
> and that will be a bargain and a debt between us. A head for a
> head, that is the game,' said he. We laughed at him and told
> him he was drunk, for how could he whip off a head when his
> own head had been whipped off? Then he began abusing us
> and calling us names, so I ran at him and cut off his head, and
> the head went on laughing where it lay, and presently he
> caught it up in his hands and ran out and plunged into the
> sea.

While Yeats has Conall tell the same tale in *The Green Helmet*,
he sustains its dramatic impetus, as he does not in *The Golden
Helmet*, through Cuchulain's comments and questions along
the way:

> *Conall.* You were gone but a little while. We were there and
>   the ale-cup full.
>   We were half drunk and merry, and midnight on the
>   stroke,

When a wise, high man came in with a red foxy cloak,
With half-shut foxy eyes and a great laughing mouth,
And he said, when we bid him drink, that he had so great
    a drouth
He could drink the sea.
Cuchulain.   I thought he had come for one of you
Out of some Connacht rath, and would lap up milk and
    mew;
But if he so loved water I have the tale awry.
Conall. You would not be so merry if he were standing by,
For when we had sung or danced as he were our next of
    kin
He promised to show us a game, the best that ever had
    been;
And when we had asked what game, he answered, 'Why,
    whip off my head!
Then one of you two stoop down, and I'll whip off his',
    he said.
'A head for a head', he said, 'that is the game that I play'.
Cuchulain. How could he whip off a head when his own had
    been whipped away?
Conall. We told him it over and over, and that ale had fud-
    dled his wit,
But he stood and laughed at us there, as though his sides
    would split,
Till I could stand it no longer, and whipped off his head
    at a blow,
Being mad that he did not answer, and more at his laugh-
    ing so,
And there on the ground where it fell it went on laughing
    at me.
Laegaire. Till he took it up in his hands—
Conall.   And splashed himself into the sea.
                                  (65–85)

That Laegaire assumes part of Conall's narrative burden reflects another of the benefits Yeats derives from fragmenting
speeches to dramatic ends. Conall and Laegaire are portrayed as
incomplete in themselves, incapable of standing individually be-

fore Cuchulain, against whom, in the blocking and dialogue, they are always paired. Yeats depicts their kind of rhetorical symbiosis immediately in *The Green Helmet* through those fourteeners with their pronounced anapestic cadence. Having seen, Laegaire supposes, "though but in the wink of an eye,/ A cat-headed man out of Connacht go pacing and spitting by" (1–2), he concludes, "But that could not be" (3); and, conditioned by the strong rhythmic pattern of his first two lines, we expect him to fill out the third, presumably explaining why that could not be. The line, however, is filled out by Conall, who in effect finishes Laegaire's thought: "You have dreamed it—there's nothing out there" (3).

Raising the curtain with this device alerts Yeats's audience from the start to the interdependence of Conall and Laegaire: the vast gap between the flawed beings they are, truncated like certain of their lines, and their pretense to having attained the heroic ideal embodied in Cuchulain. They blend finally even in mind, collaborating on their story—a stratagem Yeats had in fact exploited through Conall's reply to Cuchulain's mockery in *The Golden Helmet*:

> Conal. Why must you be always putting yourself up against Leagerie and myself? and what is more, it was no imagination at all. We said to yourselves [*sic*, ourselves?] that all came out of the flagon, and we laughed, and we said we will tell nobody about it. We made an oath to tell nobody. But twelve months after when we were sitting by this table, the flagon between us—
> Leagerie. But full up to the brim.
> Conal. The thought of that story had put us from our drinking.
> Leagerie. We were telling it over to one another.
> Conal. Suddenly that man came in with his head on his shoulders again, and the big sword in his hand. . . .

Translating prose into verse enabled Yeats to refine his treatment of Conall and Laegaire blended, dividing syntactical units, single lines between them in a stichomythic exchange. Having rebuked Cuchulain for boasting that, whatever Conall and

Laegaire may have said or done, he has "said or done a better" (90), Conall concedes, as in *The Golden Helmet*, that they too believed their tale to have come from the ale, then adds:

> And thinking that if we told it we should be a laughing stock
> Swore we should keep it secret.
> *Laegaire.*   But twelve months upon the clock—
> *Conall.* A twelvemonth from the first time—
> *Laegaire.*   And the jug full up to the brim:
> For we had been put from our drinking by the very
>   thought of him—
> *Conall.* We stood as we're standing now—
> *Laegaire.*   The horns were as empty—
> *Conall.*   When
> He ran up out of the sea with his head on his shoulders
>   again.
>   (93–97)

This dialogue, with its syncopation, looks forward to some of the parody vaudeville in Beckett (especially *Waiting for Godot*), and underscores the rationale for Yeats subtitling *The Green Helmet* "An Heroic Farce." If the subtitle seems a paradox, it embraces Cuchulain, who is genuinely heroic, as well as Conall and Laegaire, who are farcical, and suggests the source of their farcicality, which lies in their pretense to heroism.

The gap between their pretense and Cuchulain's pre-eminence, ultimately dramatized in his answer to the Red Man's challenge, is manifest in their humorlessness. Crowning Cuchulain with the emblem of his championship, the Red Man announces that he chooses "the laughing lip" (278). The lips of Conall and Laegaire never laugh. It is, indeed, by viewing themselves altogether humorlessly that they become the butts of humor. Laegaire complains of Emer that "she makes light of us" (23); Conall confesses to Cuchulain that they hide the Red Man's visit to avoid being laughed at. And they judge Cuchulain by themselves. When Cuchulain jests at the Red Man's thirst, great enough to drink the sea, Conall warns that he would be less merry were the Red Man standing by. When Cuchulain hails their fabulous adventure as "a tale worth telling" (98), Conall adds: "If you had been sitting there you had been silent like us" (102).

When the Red Man materializes, however, Cuchulain is neither silent nor solemn, addressing him as "Old herring" (114); enumerating adversaries better suited to his game, "for they are of your own sort" (118); assuring him that "If . . . no sword can harm you, I've an older trick to play,/ An old five-fingered trick" (123–24). He responds to the bargain with a light-heartedness appropriate to the spirit—"A drinking joke and a gibe and a juggler's feat, that is all" (127)—in which the Red Man claims to have proposed it. And his arrival at the house of Conall and Laegaire suggests a certain kinship between himself and the Red Man: he too has a thirst to quench.

For the Red Man emerging from the sea—that recurrent Yeatsian image of the *Anima Mundi*, the shared psychic heritage of the race—confronts not alone Cuchulain but also Conall and Laegaire with the truth of their inmost selves. Through farce distinguishing bravery from bluster, *The Green Helmet*, like all the Cuchulain plays, explores the nature of heroism. Yeats's concept of heroism has, once more, roots in Nietzsche. David S. Thatcher, tracing the growth of Nietzsche's influence in England, stresses that Nietzschean heroism is characterized by joy (German *Lust*), "dynamic exultation in the face of suffering," and nominates Cuchulain as "Yeats's most persistent embodiment" of that ideal.[10] "Not by wrath," Zarathustra declares, "but by laughter do we slay."[11] The Red Man conferring the helmet praises Cuchulain not merely because he laughs but because he "shall not turn from laughing, whatever rise or fall" (280). He epitomizes that virtue which in *The Golden Helmet* he himself, with perhaps a discreet Yeatsian nod toward Castiglione, calls "reckless." In "Poetry and Tradition," written less than a year before *The Golden Helmet*, Yeats cites Timon and Cleopatra for the fearlessness—purity he labels it in his essay—the Red Man lauds in Cuchulain; and contrasting

[10] *Nietzsche in England*, pp. 171–72 and 153.

[11] *Thus Spake Zarathustra*, trans. Thomas Common, in *The Philosophy of Nietzsche*, ed. Willard Huntington Wright (New York: Random House, 1927), p. 41.

Shakespeare's poetic heroes with traditionless "new man," he insists that, to achieve their stature, "even knowledge is not enough, for the 'recklessness' Castiglione thought necessary in good manners is necessary in this likewise, and if a man has it not he will be gloomy, and had better to his marketing again."[12]

Yeats has enlisted Castiglione in his fight against the bourgeois ethos of modern Ireland and the aesthetically sterile realism he saw it fostering. Yet he need not have gone so far as Italy, or Nietzsche's Germany, to gather support for his campaign. John O'Leary, whose death provides the point of departure for "Poetry and Tradition," condemns the bourgeoisie in *Recollections of Fenians and Fenianism* as "the lowest class morally—that is, the class influenced by the lowest motives"; and he projects his revolutionist self, whether intentionally or not, as a model of Castiglione's *sprezzatura*: "Reckless and even desperate I may, in a sense, have become; seeking, if not 'what reinforcement I might gain from hope,' at least 'what resolution from despair'. . . ."[13] Yeats treats O'Leary as a type of ideal hero, a repositor of noble tradition. As he recalls of the old Fenian in *Reveries over Childhood and Youth*, "Sometimes he would say things that would have sounded well in some heroic Elizabethan play. It became my delight to rouse him to these outbursts for I was the poet in the presence of his theme";[14] or in the famous refrain of "September 1913," "Romantic Ireland's dead and gone,/ It's with O'Leary in the grave."

O'Leary exists for Yeats as an artifact, like Timon and Cleopatra, whose "words move us because their sorrow is not their own at tomb or asp, but for all men's fate."[15] He exists as Cuchulain for those long-remembering harpers, who, the Red Man prophesies, will draw from his deeds "matter for their song" (284). While Yeats's image of O'Leary may well have usurped the place of the man in Irish history, the man, it would

---

[12] *Essays and Introductions*, p. 256.

[13] *Recollections of Fenians and Fenianism*, vol. 1 (London: Downey & Co., 1896), pp. 31 and 36.

[14] *Autobiography*, p. 64.   [15] "Poetry and Tradition," p. 255.

seem, helped to nurture the image. O'Leary's statement of personal belief—"My religion is the old Persian, to pull the bow and tell the truth"—which Yeats quotes with enthusiasm in "Poetry and Tradition" and *The Trembling of the Veil*, is lifted from Zarathustra, who remarks: " 'To speak truth, and be skilful with bow and arrow'—so seemed it alike pleasing and hard to the people from whom cometh my name—the name which is alike pleasing and hard to me."[16]

O'Leary saw himself, then—or at least encouraged Yeats to see him—as a Nietzschean figure. The parallels between him and Cuchulain in *The Green Helmet* are striking: like O'Leary an exile returned, Cuchulain offering his head to the Red Man seeks to uplift the moral consciousness of Ireland; again like O'Leary, he finds his quest repeatedly thwarted by the growing bourgeois selfhood of his countrymen. Yeats strengthens this strain in the play through his revision. In *The Golden Helmet*, when Laegaire pleads that the Young Man coming down through the rocks and hazels not be allowed to enter, Conall replies: "I will tell him to go away, for nobody must know the disgrace that is to fall upon Ireland this night." In *The Green Helmet* he replies: "He must look for his dinner elsewhere, for no one alive shall stop/ Where a shame must alight on us two before the dawn is up" (27–28).

The borders of their concern, in contrast to Cuchulain's, have shrunk from Ireland to themselves. While Conall and Laegaire each demands the helmet as his own, Cuchulain takes it "not . . . to keep it—the Red Man gave it for me,/ But I shall give it to all—to all of us three or to none" (148–49). Noble souls, says Zarathustra, "desire to have nothing gratuitously, least of all, life."[17] Conall and Laegaire desire both the Red Man's prize and life gratuitously, showing themselves of, in Nietzsche's schema, the contemptible "populace";[18] whereas Cuchulain is one of Zarathustra's "others. . . to whom life hath given itself,"

[16] *The Philosophy of Nietzsche*, p. 61. Yeats's versions of O'Leary's statement (*Essays and Introductions*, p. 247 and *Autobiography*, p. 241) differ somewhat. I have used the one from *The Trembling of the Veil* simply because it is more concise.

[17] *The Philosophy of Nietzsche*, p. 222.

[18] *Ibid.*, p. 222.

and who "are ever considering *what* [they] can best give *in return!"*[19]

Which is not to say that the Yeatsian hero constitutes himself, in anything like the ordinary political sense, a public servant. The sacrifices of Fitzgerald, Emmet, Tone are characterized in "September 1913" as "All that delirium of the brave" (22). Parnell turning from his monument in "To a Shade" "To ['happier-thoughted'] drink of that salt breath out of the sea/ When grey gulls flit about instead of men" (5–6) exhibits, in Herbert Howarth's appropriate phrase, "Shakespearean contempt" for the crowd.[20] Yeats brooding on the comparable purities of heroic and artistic motive in "Poetry and Tradition" ruminates that "It had been easier to fight, to die even, for Charles's house with Marvell's poem in the memory, but there is no zeal of service that has not been an impurity in the pure soil where the marvel grew."[21] In his translation from *The Golden Helmet* to *The Green Helmet* Cuchulain is thus relieved of his claim to be laying down his life for the peace of Ireland and his assertion that, by so doing, he is fulfilling himself.

The hero acts not by calculation but by instinct. As Yeats observes of O'Leary, "He had no self-consciousness, no visible pride and would have hated anything that could have been called a gesture, was indeed scarce artist enough to invent a gesture. . . ."[22] Hero and artist are the obverse of each other. What the hero possesses by some inexplicable alchemy of his being the artist self-consciously pursues. As Yeats again observes, by way of proposing his own law of the excluded middle, "Three types of men have made all beautiful things, Aristocracies have made beautiful manners, because their place in the world puts them above the fear of life, and the countrymen have made beautiful stories and beliefs because they have nothing to lose and so do not fear, and the artists have made all the rest, because Providence has filled them with recklessness."[23]

The artist shares in that virtue Yeats learned from O'Leary

[19] *Ibid.*, p. 222. Italics Nietzsche's.
[20] *The Irish Writers* (London: Rockliff, 1958), p. 132.
[21] *Essays and Introductions*, p. 255.
[22] *Autobiography*, pp. 141–42.   [23] "Poetry and Tradition," p. 251.

and Castiglione to regard as the key to the heroic personality. Which is to say that heroism, like the creative impulse, is first a state of mind. The contest over the helmet is a contest of wills; those episodes in "Bricriu's Feast" where Conall and Laegaire attack Cuchulain with swords, and refuse through test after test to concede his obvious superiority, Yeats omits. That Cuchulain's real trial comes from the challenge not of his fellow warriors but of a supernatural visitant establishes his Nietzschean credentials. In *Beyond Good and Evil* Nietzsche had argued:

> That which is termed "freedom of the will" is essentially the emotion of supremacy in respect to him who must obey: "I am free, 'he' must obey"—this consciousness is inherent in every will; and equally so the straining of the attention, the straight look which fixes itself exclusively on one thing, the unconditioned judgment that "this and nothing else is necessary now," the inward certainty that obedience will be rendered—and whatever else pertains to the position of the commander. A man who *wills* commands something within himself which renders obedience, or which he believes renders obedience.[24]

The Green Helmet breaks into two scenes: the first, containing the farce, in which Cuchulain demonstrates the supremacy of his will over those of Conall and Laegaire, their wives, and servants; the second, pushing farce to the verge of tragedy, in which Cuchulain faces the Red Man, proving his power to command himself.

The extreme shift in tone from the first scene to the second is signaled by the blackout and accentuated by a recurrence of the play's crucial issues. The Red Man's wager, dismissed as a joke when he leaves the helmet, becomes deadly serious when he returns. The warriors' domesticity, occasioning the catty squabble over precedence among their wives, produces the leave-taking of Emer and Cuchulain as the Red Man awaits his due. That their leave-taking repudiates the very domestic values

[24] Trans. Helen Zimmern, *The Complete Works of Friedrich Nietzsche*, ed. Oscar Levy, vol. XII (New York: Russell & Russell, 1964), p. 26, italics Nietzsche's.

marriage affirms reveals once more the Nietzschean roots to Yeats's diagnosis of society's ills. What Nietzsche called "the disease of the will" he found "worst and most varied where civilization has longest prevailed; it decreases according as 'the barbarian' still—or again—asserts his claims under the loose drapery of Western culture."[25] Though Cuchulain seeks to persuade Emer that she may profit from his death by wedding "Some kinder and comelier [more civilized] man that will sit at home in the house" (269), she prefers his wandering (barbarous) self: "Live and be faithless still" (270).

Their exchange, absent from *The Golden Helmet*, a mere moment in *The Green Helmet*, echoes the heroine's plea for life and love in *Deirdre* and is to blossom into a major theme in *The Only Jealousy of Emer* (though Emer in *The Only Jealousy*, closer to Blunt's figure in *Fand*, bespeaks the wifely prerogatives she declines in *The Green Helmet*). Like Nietzsche, Yeats continues to see in civilization, with its essentially bourgeois domestic arrangements, a force inimical to hero and artist. As the Abbey audience, versed in the Red Branch Tales, would have understood, Conall and Laegaire have lapsed from a genuinely heroic past.

It is to underscore this lapse that Yeats, through his imagery, introduces the mock-heroic dimension of the beast fable which Skene properly finds in the play.[26] If, however, Conall and Laegaire are, as Skene argues, quarrelsome roosters in mortal terror of the fox and Emer something of a hen trying to act the peacock, Cuchulain, Laeg's "cock of the yard" (164), hardly seems the conventional Chanticleer. Nor is the Red Man, "foxy" as he appears, the conventional Reynard. While Yeats, that is, suggests the presence of the beast-fable behind his scenario, he refrains from carrying the analogy through. For the incongruity inherent in the mock-heroic, and from which the farce of *The Green Helmet* arises, is largely built into the action itself: in the contrast between Conall and Laegaire and Cuchulain, in the gap between what Conall and Laegaire are and what they, and even Cuchulain, think they are. Repeating,

[25] *Ibid.*, p. 145.
[26] *The Cuchulain Plays of W.B. Yeats*, pp. 149 and 152.

but to the opposite effect, the error of Conall warning that he too would cower before the Red Man, Cuchulain judges his companions by himself. Greeted by the full flagon, the open door, the evasions of Conall and Laegaire, he concludes that "the whole thing's plain enough,/ You are waiting for some message to bring you to war or love/ In that old secret country beyond the wool-white waves,/ Or it may be down beneath them in foam-bewildered caves/ Where nine forsaken sea-queens fling shuttles to and fro" (54–58). He credits them with a taste for the heroic infidelities he has been enjoying with Aoife in "high windy Scotland" (15). And ever-ready for new adventure, he resolves that "beyond them, or beneath them, whether you will or no,/ I am going too" (59–60).

The pun on "will," implying volition as well as consent, echoes the comparable usage in Cuchulain's defiance of Laegaire—"I'll eat and sleep where I will" (42)—and reminds the audience that Conall and Laegaire are without will, without the requisite for heroic conduct. Their confrontation with Cuchulain at the door of the house dramatizes their lack, manifesting their need to make rhetoric serve for reality:

Conall. A law has been made that none shall sleep in this
    house to-night.
Young Man. Who made that law?
Conall.   We made it, and who has so good a right?
    Who else has to keep the house from the Shape-Changers
    till day?
Young Man. Then I will unmake the law, so get you out of
    the way.
        [*He pushes past Conall and goes into house.*]
Conall. I thought no living man could have pushed me from
    the door,
    Nor could any living man do it but for the dip in the
    floor;
    And had I been rightly ready there's no living man could
    do it,
    Dip or no dip.

                                (32–39)

Conall's appeal to law reflects the involvement of himself and Laegaire, as settled men, in the established society Cuchulain resists by wandering, by asserting his power to unmake laws contrary to his will. Primed with the same foreknowledge Yeats exploits to tragic ends in *Deirdre*, the audience detects the comic irony of Conall's claim to a legislative authority derived from guarding the house against Shape-Changers. And this irony is compounded in his alibi, its spuriousness clear even to an uninitiated audience, at having been pushed from the door.

A deftly structured piece of bombast, building clause by clause to its climax in his empty boast, Conall's speech underlines the cogency of Cuchulain's accusation—true beyond its author's ken—that Conall is "stuffed with pride" (52). Measured by Cuchulain, he and Laegaire are hollow men, substanceless but for pride, as the farce to which they are subjected and their rival's domination of them emphasize. Yeats accents their ironic diminution beside Cuchulain through—a device pervading the dialogue—his intricately linked rhymes. Conall's vow, "none shall sleep in this house tonight," is set against Cuchulain's to leave only after eating, sleeping, and drinking to his "heart's delight" (31), and looks toward Conall's further claim, in answer to Cuchulain's demand to know who made the law, that he and Laegaire have, "and who has so good a right?" In the conflict these lines apprehend they parallel Laegaire's determination that no man "but us two" (29) must witness the shame by dawn to afflict them, and Cuchulain's response that he will go "when the night is through" (30). This kind of pattern also, by the subtle off-rhyme of "law" with "door" and "floor," subsumes Conall's two, equally awry pretensions to noble stature, that he possesses not only the physical prowess required for standing up to the true hero but the moral power needed to legislate for his world.

To the acute ears among Yeats's audience, then, sound reinforces sense in projecting the struggle between Cuchulain and his adversaries and in presaging its outcome. From his entrance to the arrival of the Red Man, Cuchulain directs the action: his mastery over his companions at the door to the house thus foreshadows the whole first scene. When Conall alerts them to the signs of the Red Man's approach, Cuchulain arranges their defense; when the Red Man appears, Cuchulain confronts him. When he leaves the helmet, Cuchulain turns it "into a cup of peace" (189). When the Charioteers, Stable Boys, and Scullions run in shouting and drowning each other's voices with horns, Cuchulain restores order; when the wives take up the argument, he moves to pacify them.

And when the Red Man returns demanding his debt, the play's focus narrows to himself, Cuchulain, and Emer. Conall and Laegaire, their wives, the servants shrink to mere stage props. The story Conall has begun to tell Cuchulain becomes Cuchulain's story; for he alone is willing to see it out to the end.

Rendering the play the last chapter of a tale told as prelude to the scenario is a strategy Yeats had introduced earlier, through the Blind Man in *On Baile's Strand* and the Musicians in *Deirdre*, and which—stressing his absorption in the mythmaking process—is to emerge as one of his dramatic signatures in the Cuchulain cycle. The Red Man arrives at "midnight on the stroke" (66), not only the witching hour but the instant, neither night nor day, simulating (as it will again years later in "Byzantium," where "At midnight on the Emperor's pavement flit/ Flames that no faggot feeds" [25–26]) art's removal from time. The vantage is that of the supernatural being, the Red Man himself, who, transcending history, comprehends history: who, like Blake's Bard, "Present, Past, & Future sees" and so prophesies the day—in which Yeats and his audience live— "When heart and mind shall darken that the weak may end the strong" (453).

In the collaboration of hero and artist lies the potential for building a defense against the inevitability of that day. If less assertively and brilliantly then "Byzantium," *The Green Helmet* too proclaims the magical power of imagination to escape the tyranny of time and place, of mortality. Though Cuchulain passes, he is preserved by the songs of the long-remembering harpers.

That Yeats looked upon himself as one of those harpers and his work as contributing to their corpus of song is suggested by a rhetorical question posed in "The Play, the Player, and the Scene" and virtually anticipating *The Green Helmet*: "What is there left for us, that have seen the newly discovered stability of things changed from an enthusiasm to a weariness, but to labour with a high heart, though it may be with weak hands, to rediscover an art of the theatre that shall be joyful, fantastic, whimsical, beautiful, resonant, and altogether reckless?" Yeats appears to be proposing a program in which farce may itself serve as an antidote to the decadence he perceives around him. Yet he appears convinced too that, in the face of the world's weariness, the poet's weakness, farce must inevitably give way to tragedy. "The arts," he adds, "are at their greatest when they seek for a life growing always more scornful of everything that is not itself and passing into its own fullness, as it were, even more completely as all that is created out of the passing mode of society slips from it; and attaining that fullness, perfectly it may be—and from this is tragic joy and the perfectness of tragedy—when the world itself has slipped away in death."[27] Having finished *The Green Helmet*, Yeats was not to write another Cuchulain play for six years. When he returned to the cycle, it was in a tragic form designed—aesthetically and commercially—to achieve fullness independent of a world which, wracked by the Great War and in Dublin the special horror of the Easter Rising, seemed surely slipping away in death.

[27] *Explorations*, pp. 169–70.

V

In the Eye of the Mind

Proclaiming in "Certain Noble Plays of Japan" his invention of the new dramatic form shaping *At the Hawk's Well*, Yeats stresses of his accomplishment that it "can be played in a room for so little money that forty or fifty readers of poetry can pay the price"; that it has, as he adds, "no need of mob or Press [instruments of the hated bourgeoisie] to pay its way."[1] What he is attributing to himself is the invention not alone of a theatrical mode but of a theater, like the theater he thought he had seen growing from the Shakespeare festival at Stratford, "made not to make money, but for the pleasure of making it."[2]

The reduction of conventional theater to something made not for the pleasure of making it but to make money, Yeats habitually traced to naturalism, which, by vulgarizing the drama, also vulgarized its audience. In his Preface to the first version of *At the Hawk's Well*, published in *Harper's Bazaar* for March, 1917, he tells of sitting behind a husband, wife, and woman companion during a performance of *The King's Threshold* at the Court Theatre in London. The woman friend finds her attention roused by the red costumes of the princesses. "The distinguished painter who had designed the clothes at any rate could interest her." The wife, who may be, Yeats speculates, a reader of his poetry, leaves announcing that she " 'would not have missed it for the world'." Her husband is simply bored. Yet, Yeats concludes his story, when he thinks of his play, he calls to mind neither the enthusiastic wife nor "even her friend who found the long red gloves of the little princesses amusing, but always that bored man. . . ."[3]

Though escaping bored men has led him, he observes, presumably commenting, again in his Preface for *Harper's Bazaar*, on the dramatic barrenness of the years between *The Green*

[1] *Essays and Introductions*, p. 221.
[2] "At Stratford-on-Avon," *Essays and Introductions*, p. 96.
[3] *Variorum Plays*, p. 415.

Helmet in 1910 and *At the Hawk's Well* in 1916, "to shrink from sending [his] muses where they are but half-welcomed," he reiterates that he believes himself a dramatist, and needs a theater, accounting for his delay in discovering one appropriate to his talent by his failure to realize "in my youth that my theatre must be the ancient theatre that can be made by unrolling a carpet or marking out a place with a stick, or setting a screen against the wall." Emphasizing that he has at last found his model for such a theater in *Noh*, he cites as almost the primary virtue of *Noh* its lack of elaborately realistic stage backdrops and settings: "I do not think of my discovery as mere economy, for it has been a great gain to get rid of scenery, to substitute for a crude landscape painted upon canvas three performers who, sitting before the wall or a patterned screen, describe landscape or event, and accompany movement with drum and gong, or deepen the emotion of the words with zither or flute."[4]

Eliminating or at least minimizing scenery is hardly a dramatic stratagem Yeats came to by way of Japan. Suggested to him partly by the conditions of the Elizabethan theater, it is manifest as an ideal in the platform stage for which he wrote *On Baile's Strand*. And writing *On Baile's Strand* for a platform stage expresses a conscious Yeatsian reaction against naturalistic scene design, which, to him, epitomized the aesthetic bankruptcy of commercial theater, and which he pilloried in "At Stratford-on-Avon" as a trade rather than an art.

His attack on the stage-painter's efforts to simulate nature in "At Stratford-on-Avon" is, moreover, a coda of sorts to the argument of "The Theatre," two years earlier, locating in the rise of naturalism the fall of the theater of art:

> As audiences and actors changed, managers learned to substitute meretricious landscapes, painted upon wood and canvas, for the descriptions of poetry, until the painted scenery, which had in Greece been a charming explanation of what was least important in the story, became as important as the story. It needed some imagination, some gift for day-dreams,

4 *Ibid.*, pp. 415–16.

to see the horses and the fields and flowers of Colonus as one
listened to the elders gathered about Oedipus, or to see 'the
pendant bed and cradle' of the 'martlet' as one listened to
Banquo before the castle of Macbeth; but it needs no imagination to admire the painting of one of the more obvious effects of nature painted by somebody who understands how to
show everything to the most hurried glance. At the same
time the managers made the costumes of the actors more and
more magnificent that the mind might sleep in peace, while
the eye took pleasure in the magnificence of velvet and silk
and in the physical beauty of women. These changes gradually perfected the theater of commerce, the masterpiece of
that movement towards externality in life and thought and
art against which the criticism of our day is learning to protest.[5]

The conditions against which the criticism of our day, vintage
1900, is learning to protest are precisely those repudiated six-
teen years later through the dramatic vehicle of *At the Hawk's
Well*. The friends Yeats evokes in his *Harper's Bazaar* Preface
as the audience for *At the Hawk's Well*—to whom painted
scenery is unnecessary, because their "imagination kept living
by the arts can imagine a mountain covered with thorn-trees in
a drawing room without any great trouble"—are the opposites
of that other audience, admiring a painting of one of the more
obvious effects of nature, their minds sleeping while their eyes
take pleasure in the magnificence of velvet and silk and in the
physical beauty of women. His friends enjoy some gift for day-
dreams; they are analogous to the few for whom, as he learned
from Ezra Pound, the *Noh* was written: "those trained to catch
the allusion."[6]

Training to catch the allusion opened the Japanese audience,
by Pound's lights, to the same kind of aesthetic experience
Yeats sought to induce in the audience of *At the Hawk's Well*.
"The reader," Pound warns, suggesting that he must project
himself as far as possible into the situation of a watcher at the

[5] *Essays and Introductions*, p. 169.

[6] Ezra Pound and Ernest Fenollosa, *The Classic Noh Theatre of Japan* (New
York: New Directions, 1959), p. 4.

play, "will miss the feel of suspense if he is unable to put himself in sympathy with the priest eager to see 'even in vision' the beauty lost in the years, 'the shadow of the past in bright form'."[7] To submit to the power of *Noh* is to expand one's consciousness, as one's consciousness is expanded by seeing the horses, the fields and flowers around Colonus; or by seeing " 'the pendant bed and procreant cradle' " of the " 'martlet' " before Macbeth's castle; or by seeing the choked well and stripped boughs toward which the ivory faced man climbs.

In the radical simplicity of *At the Hawk's Well*, that is, Yeats finally devised a method for restoring the imaginations and awakening the minds of his audience. Ernest Fenollosa, in his contribution to the theoretical context he and Pound built for their translations, asserts that "the poetic sweetness or poignancy" of what he calls the "primary human relation or emotion" each *Noh* drama crystallizes "is carried to its highest degree by carefully excluding all such obtuse elements as mimetic realism or vulgar sensation might demand."[8] Yeats appropriates this view to his own use, insisting in "Certain Noble Plays of Japan" that "imaginative art," as distinct from its drear "unimaginative" rival, maintains its distance from life: "and this distance, once chosen, must be firmly held against a pushing world. Verse, ritual, music, and dance in association with action require that gesture, facial expression, stage arrangement must help in keeping the door."[9]

A method of keeping the door was what Yeats had, years earlier at the performance of *Dido and Aeneas* he lauds in his essay on Shakespeare, thought he had found in Craig's stagecraft. "You have," he wrote to Craig, "created a new art"; and, defining the magnitude of that creation, he was to declare in "At Stratford-on-Avon" that it called to the audience's eyes "an ideal country where everything was possible, even speaking in verse, or speaking to music, or the expression of the whole life in dance. . . ."[10]

---

[7] *Ibid.*, pp. 26–27.   [8] *Ibid.*, p. 69.   [9] *Essays and Introductions*, p. 224.

[10] *Essays and Introductions*, pp. 100–101. The letter to Craig is quoted in Alan Tomlinson, "W.B. Yeats and Gordon Craig," *Ariel* (Calgary), III (1972), 52.

At the Hawk's Well goes Craig one better: calling to the audience's eyes an ideal country not through decorative as opposed to mimetic scenery but through the absence of scenery,
its replacement by language and (devices Craig also used) mask
and dance. Recounting in "Certain Noble Plays" his inspection
of Cuchulain's mask and headdress at Edmund Dulac's studio,
Yeats confides his hope that the actor in the role "will appear
perhaps like an image seen in reverie by some Orphic worship-
per," and that, as the playwright, he himself will "have attained the distance from life which can make credible strange
events, elaborate words."[11]

These desires, essentially statements of his aims in *At the
Hawk's Well*, not only recall Pound's characterization of *Noh* at
its best as "an image"—"built up about it as the Greek plays are
built up about a single moral conviction"[12]—but echo Yeats's
own praise of Craig's *Dido and Aeneas*. If Yeats's ideas of
dramaturgy have been altered by his encounter with *Noh*, his
ideas of what drama should do have not. Of Ito's performance
in Lady Cunard's drawing room, he observes: "There, where
no studied lighting, no stage-picture made an artificial world,
he was able, as he rose from the floor, where he had been sitting
cross-legged, or as he threw out an arm, to recede from us into
some more powerful life." Through the distance his dance effects between himself as Guardian of the Well and the mundane
lives lived by his audience, he becomes for Yeats a "tragic image" out of *Anima Mundi*, a figure inhabiting "the deeps of the
mind."[13]

That Yeats wished the play overall viewed as he viewed Ito
dancing the Guardian is established by the Musicians' opening
song, which not only sets the action in "the eye of the mind"
but also takes the form of a conjuration: its singers calling forth
from the void (another reason for the empty stage) Cuchulain,
the Old Man, and the mountainside with its rocks, choked well,
and bare trees. In proclaiming, years before in "Magic," the
evocative power of symbols, Yeats had suggested that those

[11] *Essays and Introductions*, p. 221.
[12] Pound and Fenollosa, *Classic Noh Theatre*, p. 37.
[13] "Certain Noble Plays," p. 224.

same mysterious currents, harnessed consciously by "the masters of magic," are at work half unconsciously in the formulations of "their successors, the poet, the musician and the artist."[14] The kinship he perceives between magician and poet, musician, or artist—conjurers of images all—adumbrates the varieties of creative experience detailed in *Per Amica Silentia Lunae*, and underlies *At the Hawk's Well*. Refusing in *Per Amica* to distinguish among images—appearances fashioned by the individual mind or apparitions transported from the beyond—arguing essentially that no distinction exists, Yeats professes himself a kind of medium (though the implicit corollary to this profession, that his art has about it the character of seance, is not wholly to surface until November 17, 1930, when there unfolds upon the Abbey stage a Yeatsian seance indeed, *The Words upon the Window-Pane*).

Yeats, however, had been wrestling with the problems attached to bringing the *Anima Mundi* and its spirit inhabitants to concretion in the theater at least since his enthusiasm for Shakespeare's histories had started him meditating his own heroic cycle. "Mr. Benson did not venture to play the scene in Richard III where the ghosts walk as Shakespeare wrote it," he reports of the production at Stratford, "but had his scenery been as simple as Mr. Gordon Craig's purple back-cloth that made Dido and Aeneas seem wandering on the edge of eternity, he would have found nothing absurd in pitching the tents of Richard and Richmond side by side." Yeats thus recognizes from the beginning that the ultimate realism demands separation from reality. To his criticism of Benson's direction, he appends Goethe's pronouncement, invoked again in praise of the Bernhardt-De Max *Phedra*, that "Art is art, because it is not nature," adding by way of elaboration: "It brings us near to the archetypal ideas themselves, and away from nature, which is but their looking-glass."[15]

Bringing us near the archetypal ideas was, Yeats believed, the achievement of the great Elizabethan drama. Describing the conditions under which it thrived in terms suggesting his own

[14] *Essays and Introductions*, p. 49.
[15] "At Stratford-on-Avon," p. 101–102.

Ireland, he observes in the Introduction to his *Poems of Spenser* (1906) that "The dramatists lived in a disorderly world, reproached by many, persecuted even, but following their imagination wherever it led them. Their imagination, driven hither and thither by beauty and sympathy, put on something of the nature of eternity. Their subject was always the soul, the whimsical, self-awakening, self-exciting, self-appeasing soul. They celebrated its heroical, passionate will going by its own path to immortal and invisible things."[16] Yeats looking at the Elizabethan drama—and this a full decade before *At the Hawk's Well*—sees in its patterns of character and action what he is to see in *Noh*, even to Pound's claim that the plays typically focus on "some one going a journey."[17] The *Noh*-like aura Yeats finds in the Elizabethans generally he finds in Shakespeare particularly, whose kings, queens, warring nobles, insurgent courtiers, and people of the gutter have "been to me almost too visible, too audible, too full of an unearthly energy. . . . The people my mind's eye have seen have too much of the extravagance of dreams, like all the inventions of art before our crowded life had brought moderation and compromise, to seem more than a dream, and yet all else has grown dim before them."[18]

While troubled by what he felt to be the excessive luxuriance of Shakespeare's style, Yeats discovered in his plays an overpowering instance of the psyche given dramatic life. In the starkness of their stage arrangements, their stress on poetry, Yeats's adaptations of *Noh* reach not only out toward aristocratic Japan but also back toward Elizabethan England. Reconstructing in "First Principles" what he thought must be Shakespeare's, and knew to be his own, way of arriving at subjects for drama, Yeats hypothesizes that "One day, as he sat over Holinshed's *History of England*, he persuaded himself that Richard II, with his French culture, 'his too great friendliness to his friends', his beauty of mind, and his fall before dry, repelling Bolingbroke, would be a good image for an accustomed

---

[16] "Edmund Spenser," *Essays and Introductions*, p. 370.
[17] Pound and Fenollosa, *Classic Noh Theatre*, p. 12.
[18] "At Stratford-on-Avon," p. 97.

mood of fanciful, impracticable lyricism in his own mind."[19] Shakespeare too was writing psychic allegory, masked autobiography, for which the historical circumstances of his plots served as convenient organizing fictions. As Yeats, once more quoting Goethe, whom he labels "the founder of historical drama in Germany," emphasizes of the playwright dramatizing history, " 'We do the people of history the honour of naming after them the creations of our own minds.' "[20]

Though the existence of Cuchulain remains in doubt, *At the Hawk's Well* and the rest of the cycle to which it belongs are— like its models from *Noh* and the cycles to which they belong—kinds of historical drama, attempts to capture the ambiance, as Yeats imagined it, of Ireland's heroic age; its characters are creations of his mind. To the degree that these plays concern not only crises in their lives but also the playwright's way of thinking about them, in effect of creating them, they show how, for Yeats, heroic and aesthetic experience merge. *At the Hawk's Well* dramatizes this merging. Through the quasi-*Noh* vehicle shaping its scenario, Yeats achieves what he thought Shakespeare had achieved, yet what his own partly Shakespearean mode in *On Baile's Strand* precluded: an extended reverie in the theater. As Richard Ellmann pointed out long ago, the conclusion to *Reveries over Childhood and Youth*—"All life weighed in the scales of my own life seems to me a preparation for something that never happens"—Yeats had once considered as curtain lines to *At the Hawk's Well*. He ends his preliminary draft, then called *The Well of Immortality*, with the choric lament: "Accursed the life of man. Between passion and emptiness what he longs for never comes. All his days are a preparation for what never comes."[21]

Written in 1914, published in 1915, *Reveries over Childhood and Youth* is what its title suggests: both a narrative of events

[19] *Explorations*, p. 145.
[20] "First Principles," p. 144.
[21] *The Man and the Masks*, p. 216. See also Curtis B. Bradford, *Yeats at Work* (Carbondale, Illinois: Southern Illinois University Press, 1965), p. 181. Bradford reproduces the several draft versions in his chapter on *At the Hawk's Well*.

and a meditation, a reverie, on the growth of the poet's mind. Yeats surely recognized the implications for *At the Hawk's Well*, begun as *Reveries* was being published, of transferring a deeply personal statement from his autobiography to the Musicians' closing song. His suppression of this statement may reflect an effort to lead his audience from a narrowly autobiographical, and so damagingly reductive, understanding of the play. That he has not altogether succeeded Ellmann and Wilson demonstrate: the one observing that, as the Old Man has been waiting by the well fifty years, Yeats was fifty when he wrote the play; the other seizing on the symbolism of impotence inherent in the constellation of choked well, Old Man, and waste locale to argue that the scenario projects the failure of Yeats's love for Maud Gonne.[22]

Yeats is interested in dramatizing his own tribulations and conflicts, however, only to the extent that they mirror general human experience. "It is one of the most inexplicable things about human nature," he asserts in "First Principles," "that a writer, with a strange temperament, an Edgar Allan Poe, let us say, made what he is by conditions that never existed before, can create personages and lyric emotions which startle us by being at once bizarre and an image of our own secret thoughts. Are we not face to face with the microcosm, mirroring everything in universal Nature?" Yeats makes Poe his example as, obviously, the strangest of temperaments, capable of the most bizarre of personages and emotions. If we find in him an image of our own secret thoughts, Yeats's theory of artistic communication is confirmed: "It is no more necessary for the characters created by a romance writer, or a dramatist, to have existed before, than for his own personality to have done so; characters and personality alike, as is perhaps true in the instance of Poe, may draw half their life not from the solid earth but from some dreamy drug."[23]

Yeats's experiment with *Noh* is at least roughly analogous to his use of Poe for showing how writer and reader connect.

[22] *The Man and the Masks*, p. 215; *Yeats's Iconography*, p. 30.
[23] *Explorations*, p. 144.

While he could hardly have chosen a form more foreign to his audience, he renders it a gripping instrument for drowning those dykes between himself and them. Having, by words uttered against the backdrop of a bare stage, induced them to participate in painting the scene, he specifies that the Old Man and Young Man enter *"through the audience."* For they are psychically of the audience. "The greatest art," Yeats had declared in *Samhain* for 1905, "symbolises not those things that we have observed so much as those things that we have experienced, and when the imaginary saint or lover or hero moves us most deeply, it is the moment when he awakens within us for an instant our own heroism, our own sanctity, our own desire."[24] What the audience sees upon the stage mirrors, idealized, their best (or worst) selves.

Old Man and Young Man are thus described by the Musicians—given existence in the audience's mind's eye—before their identities begin to emerge through drama. The Young Man is woven into the unfolding landscape: "I call to the mind's eye/ Pallor of an ivory face,/ Its lofty dissolute air,/ A man climbing up to a place/ The salt sea wind has swept bare" (4–8). The Old Man is announced through the essential fact of his past—that he "has been watching by his well/ These fifty years" (40–41)—and a word-picture of the action he pantomimes as he crouches to build his fire: "He has made a little heap of leaves;/ He lays the dry sticks on the leaves/ And, shivering with cold, he has taken up/ The fire-stick and socket from its hole./ He whirls it round to get a flame;/ And now the dry sticks take the fire,/ And now the fire leaps up and shines/ Upon the hazels and the empty well" (45–52).

The pantomime, conducted in movements like a marionette's; the accompanying narrative, almost without need of pantomimist to fill out its scene; the ivory—that is sculpted or mask-like—face of the climbing Cuchulain, all draw attention to the artifice of the play as artifice. And Yeats's revisions seem partly made to strengthen this focus. Throughout the manuscripts, and in the printed texts preceding *Four Plays for Danc-*

[24] *Ibid.*, p. 196.

ers (1921), the Musicians refer to the well by which the Old Man watches not as "his well" but "this well."[25] The change, small as it is, reinforces the sense that the well, indeed the whole landscape and its inhabitants, exist as an emanation of the consciousness registering them. They are perceived differently by the Musicians, who are afraid; the Old Man, who seeks there eternal life; and Cuchulain, who finds the immortality conferred by myth. In Coleridge's formulation, "O Lady! we receive but what we give,/ And in our life alone does Nature live."

Through the Old Man, who waits, and the Young Man, who wanders, then, Yeats confronts the audience with the contrary possibilities in themselves. The Old Man has undergone the adventure the Young Man is living: "I came like you/ When young in body and in mind, and blown/ By what had seemed to me a lucky sail./ The well was dry, I sat upon its edge,/ I waited the miraculous flood, I waited/ While the years passed and withered me away" (128–33). The suggestion implicit in this disclosure, that Old Man and Young Man embody phases in an endless cycle of human experience, is plainly asserted in Yeats's prose draft: "Fifty and more years ago I came hither, as young as you are, my hair upon my shoulders and a spear in my hand. The well was dry and I sat down and waited. I knew—one had told me as [I] tell you—that it filled at some secret hour."[26] Such details have led Moore to conclude that *At the Hawk's Well* dismisses the heroic enterprise as illusory: the Old Man is what the Young Man must become.[27]

But Yeats altered the Old Man's recollection, eliminating the presumably even older man who tells the adventurer, as he in turn tells Cuchulain, of the secret hour when the water flows; and Cuchulain himself breaks the cycle. The curse he accepts by gazing into the Guardian's unmoistened eyes is not the curse of age, with which the Old Man is already burdened. That Cuchul-

[25] See not only the *Variorum* but also Bradford, *Yeats at Work*, pp. 183, 196, and 212.

[26] Bradford, *Yeats at Work*, p. 178.

[27] "Cuchulain, Christ and the Queen of Love: Aspects of Yeatsian Drama," *Tulane Drama Review*, VI (1962), 152.

ain chooses, as the artist chooses—as, Yeats implies, all men must choose—between courses, if not curses, is established by the Musicians. "The heart would be always awake," sings the Second Musician, and then, stating with equal force the obverse of this proposition, "The heart would turn to its rest" (19–20). Helen Vendler, identifying the voices echoed by the Musician in these lines (as she has in the Musicians' songs throughout the play), traces the first to Cuchulain, the second to the Old Man.[28] While the aspiration toward perpetual waking is clearly expressed in Cuchulain's questing spirit, as the desire for rest in the Old Man's easeful waiting, this neat division of the heart's moods seems to me oversimple. The prospect of immortality, also imaged in the eternally wakeful heart, has drawn them both. The promise of death, imaged in the heart at rest, shadows them both. Yeats has wrought the Musicians' songs to reflect an admixture of the moods actuating his principals, with sometimes one, sometimes the other dominant, emphasizing their function as aspects of an encompassing, archetypal mind posing action against contemplation, life against death.

Which is one way of defining the reverie the play stages. Sequentially and logically, its scenario proceeds from the Musicians' question triggered by their glimpse of that "lofty dissolute" (6) figure climbing toward the well, "What were his life soon done!/ Would he lose by that or win?" (9–10). To this question, the Musicians supply their own answer, in the process adumbrating the whole symbolic thrust of the drama: "A mother that saw her son/ Doubled over a speckled shin,/ Cross-grained with ninety years,/ Would cry, 'How little worth/ Were all my hopes and fears/ And the hard pain of his birth!' " (11–16). It is among the commonplaces of Yeats criticism that these lines look forward, thematically and metaphorically, to "Among School Children." "Among School Children" too is a reverie, in descriptive-meditative form, affirming after long torment art's transcendence of time and change.

The poem substantially repeats the focus of the play, but through the more traditional strategies of the Romantic ode. As

[28] *Yeats's VISION and the Later Plays*, p. 208.

the children in the schoolroom evoke for Yeats's persona "a Ledaean body" (presumably Maud Gonne in her youthful beauty), which in turn calls to his mind's eye "Her present image . . . Hollow of cheek as though it drank the wind/ And took a mess of shadows for its meat" (9 and 25–28), the Young Man in quest of what must inevitably elude him provokes the Musicians to their bitter rejection of the worth of long life, which then crystallizes in the Old Man, embodying the fate the Young Man must suffer should he repeat the Old Man's folly. Behind both sequences stands the artist, wrestling with the inevitability of his own imaginative and physical decay. In "Among School Children" his involvement is made overt by his public self, re-emerging midway through the monologue to dismiss the unfulfilled dreams of his youth: "And I though never of Ledaean kind/ Had pretty plumage once—enough of that,/ Better to smile on all that smile, and show/ There is a comfortable kind of old scarecrow" (29–32). In *At the Hawk's Well* his involvement is established indirectly, through the framing device of the Musicians' songs, inviting us to view Old Man and Young Man as images, given visual presence by actors translating word into gesture, and—a technique Yeats had used in *Deirdre*—the reinforcement of this device through the blending of character into the metaphorical substructure of the play.

In their barrenness the Old Man and the landscape mirror each other.[29] The hazel leaves are withered; the years have withered the Old Man. "He is all doubled up with age;/ The old thorn-trees are doubled so" (42–43). And bent double, he realizes dramatically the Musicians' figure of the ninety-year-old mother's son. Yeats would have us see him not only as an image held in the mind's eye but also as an emanation from the deeps of that mind. *At the Hawk's Well* stages the dynamics of its own composition.

To this end, Yeats renders Cuchulain, as he had Deirdre and Naoise, aware of acting the hero's role in a myth. When the

---

[29] Edna G. Sharoni in a recent article, "*At the Hawk's Well*: Yeats's Unresolved Conflict Between Language and Silence," *Comparative Drama*, 7 (1973), 164, argues that the withered landscape describes the furnishings of the Old Man's soul.

Old Man asks what mischief brings him, he answers: "A rumour has led me,/ A story told over the wine toward dawn./ I rose from table, found a boat, spread sail,/ And with a lucky wind under the sail/ Crossed waves that have seemed charmed, and found this shore" (89–93). The play comprises the last chapter of that story, as *Deirdre* comprises the last chapter of the story begun by its First Musician. Living the story and writing it become analogous experiences.

Yeats, indeed, recurrently employs the metaphor of voyaging, with Byzantium in the end emerging as his ultimate port of call, to project the artist's quest for his image. Probing the hostility between bourgeois puritanism and the arts in "At Stratford-on-Avon," he argues that "The accusation of Sin produced its necessary fruit, hatred of all that was abundant, extravagant, exuberant, of all that sets a sail for shipwreck. . . ." Summing up his hopes for the new form announced in "Certain Noble Plays of Japan," he proclaims his confidence that his "writings if they be seaworthy will put to sea, and I cannot tell where they will be carried by the wind."[30] This mode of imagery may well manifest the avatar of Shelley, risen once more from the psychic depths in which Yeats's early enthusiasm had enshrined him. In "The Philosophy of Shelley's Poetry" Yeats had speculated that Shelley's first poems reveal his subconscious laying hands on "the rudder of his imagination," and had portrayed him obsessed with "a vision of a boat drifting down a broad river between high hills where there were caves and towers, and following the light of one Star. . . ."[31] The portrayal suggests, as George Bornstein points out, the Poet of *Alastor*, who, like Cuchulain seeking the Well of Immortality, entrusts himself to sea and wind in his search for the veiled maid of his dream.[32]

Alastor beautifully exemplifies Bloom's definition of internalized quest romance. In Shelley's own commentary on the poem, "It represents a youth of uncorrupted feelings and adventurous genius led forth by an imagination inflamed and

---

[30] *Essays and Introductions*, pp. 105 and 237.

[31] *Ibid.*, pp. 78 and 94–95.

[32] *Yeats and Shelley* (Chicago: University of Chicago Press, 1970), p. 43.

purified through familiarity with all that is excellent and majestic, to the contemplation of the universe. He drinks deep of the fountains of knowledge, and is still insatiate."[33]

Alastor and *At the Hawk's Well* are akin, each, as Bloom suggests, epitomizing in its own way what he calls the hero's parable: "One can burn to the socket, or pursue the poet's fate, questing after the dream while shadowed by the *alastor*, avenger and dark brother."[34] He is paraphrasing the conclusion to Shelley's Preface (actually lines quoted from Wordsworth's *Excursion*), in which precisely these alternatives are posed: " 'The good die first,/ And those whose hearts are dry as summer dust,/ Burn to the socket!' " Shelley's hero in a sense does both, embracing the whole of human experience. While he is of the good who die first, pursuing the poet's fate, the pursuit debilitates him, as time would: it burns him to the socket. Addressing the stream he follows toward death, he says, "Thou imagest my life" (505). In imaging his life the stream symbolizes the acceleration in aging brought on by the quest: "For, as fast years flow away,/ The smooth brow gathers, and the hair grows thin/ And white, and where irradiate dewy eyes/ Had shown, gleam stony orbs:—so from his steps/ Bright flowers departed, and the beautiful shade/ Of the green groves, with all their odorous winds/ And musical motions" (533–39). Having been hurtled along the cascading river almost into the abyss, the Poet finds his hair "withered" (413). Studying his reflection in a well, he observes his eyes "wan," his hair "thin" (467–71). Or, as *Ille* asks *Hic* in the debate of *"Ego Dominus Tuus,"* written all but in tandem with *At the Hawk's Well*, "What portion in the world can the artist have/ Who has awakened from the common dream/ But dissipation and despair?" (49–51).

Old Man and Young Man are not, that is, mutually exclusive personalities. By the last play in the cycle, Yeats has shifted his focus, wrenching the original myth, to show Cuchulain grown old. For the mind imagining them into being, the attitudes each embodies are equally facets of a lived reality. The Old Man enacts the contemplative state, and he pays the contemplative's,

---

[33] Preface to *Alastor*, *The Complete Works of Percy Bysshe Shelley*, vol. I, p. 173.

[34] *Yeats*, p. 298.

the poet's, price. As Cuchulain remarks of him, "You seem as dried up as the leaves and sticks,/ As though you had no part in life" (181–82).

Having paid the poet's price, however, he misses the poet's reward. In *The Trembling of the Veil* Yeats, summing up his contributions to the meetings of the Rhymers' Club, complains of himself that "I was full of thought, often very abstract thought, longing all the while to be full of images. . . ."[35] The Old Man too, incorporating this essentially self-destructive side of the poet's nature, is full of abstract thought, dividing mind from body, denying unity of being. Craving human companionship, he pleads with the Guardian—and these are his first words in the play—"Why don't you speak to me?" (57). Recognizing in her silence, her glassy stare, signs of an impending flow of water in the well, he asks about the subject on which he would most have her speak: "Do you know anything?" (72). Both are the wrong questions. Speech, knowledge imply abstraction, whereas the Guardian eschews abstraction. When she speaks, she offers only trivia, observations on the weather; when she expresses herself meaningfully, she dances, thinks with her body. And Yeats finally is to write this implicit uneasiness with the materials of his craft into an explicit indictment, uttered by the producer of *The Death of Cuchulain*, who in his prefatory monologue promises a dance as a way of averting the spoilage attendant on words.

Words spoil because they require intellectual response. Unlike dance, incapable of direct apprehension by an audience, they cannot, for Yeats at least, be sensed, even under the magical hand of the greatest of poets, as immediately as the odor of a rose. In the eyes of the audience they drive a wedge between the artist and his art. As Cuchulain must repudiate the Old Man's goal of personal immortality, and the contemplative stance by which he seeks its attainment, for the immortality of myth, to be attained through the heroism of the quest, he must also in preparing to undertake the quest grasp the inadequacy of words. He too has set sail, meaning to drink from the well and live forever; he too asks the Guardian, in effect, whether she knows anything. Arriving to his predecessor's anguish that "It

[35] *Autobiography*, p. 112.

is enough to drive an old man crazy/ To look all day upon these broken rocks,/ And ragged thorns, and that one stupid face,/ And speak and get no answer," he replies: "Then speak to me" (73–76). The demand seems addressed equally to the Old Man and the Guardian; and both in their own ways speak to him: the Old Man in conversation, the Guardian in dance.

The Old Man speaks to him, however, of cowardice and cupidity, while the Guardian draws him irrevocably onto the perilous path. That the Old Man has never heard Cuchulain's name attests to his retreat not merely from the world but from the ennobling enterprise to which Cuchulain gives his life. That Yeats weighed the impression the Old Man's ignorance would leave is suggested by the lateness in the evolution of the play at which it is introduced. In the prose draft the Old Man exclaims at Cuchulain's announcement of himself, "That violent and turbulent man." Even in the initial verse draft, where their meeting is rendered in what is almost its finished form, he remarks: "I have [heard] that name about a shepherd's fire."[36] In both, moreover, as in the version performed and published, he reacts to Cuchulain's appearance with fear: "you are like those/ Who are crazy for the shedding of men's blood,/ And for the love of women" (87–89). By the pragmatic lights motivating the Old Man, Cuchulain seems mad, as he seems to Conchubar and his subsidiary kings.

The Old Man is a foil to Cuchulain, much as Laegaire and Conall are. Though, in tone, *At the Hawk's Well* turns *The Green Helmet* on its head, the Old Man's anxiety that Cuchulain will cheat him of his drink ("O get you gone,/ At any moment now I shall hear it bubble" [195–96]) elicits the same sort of characteristic responses—magnanimity in Cuchulain, selfhood in the Old Man—as the quarrel over the Red Man's prize:[37]

> *Young Man.* I'll take it in my hands. We shall both drink
> And even if there are but a few drops,
> Share them.

[36] Bradford, *Yeats at Work*, pp. 178 and 185.

[37] Skene, *Cuchulain Plays*, p. 140, notes the apparent echo of *The Green Helmet* in Cuchulain's words.

Old Man. But swear that I may drink the first;
    The young are greedy, and if you drink the first
    You'll drink it all. . . .

                                      (201–205)

Yeats had, in fact, originally intended Cuchulain to propose catching the water in his helmet, to share with the Old Man as he shares the ale, and so the trophy itself, with Laegaire and Conall.[38]

And like them, the Old Man provides a measure of Cuchulain's superiority. When Cuchulain decides to await the water, the Old Man pleads with him: "No! Go from this accursed place!" (124). When he vows to pierce his foot rather than sleep, the Old Man protests as if the agony would be his own: "No, do not pierce it, for the foot is tender,/ It feels pain much" (143–44). When he determines to face Aoife, the Old Man again pleads: "O, do not go! The mountain is accursed;/ Stay with me, I have nothing more to lose,/ I do not now deceive you" (246–48).

In each case Cuchulain makes the heroic choice against the Old Man's counsel of timidity. Together, these choices trace a transformation in Cuchulain's consciousness, phases in the growth of his commitment to the hero's way, from kinship between him and the Old Man, both seekers of eternal life, to ascendancy over the Old Man, for whom pain as an antidote to the dancers' spell is unendurable, to outright repudiation of personal immortality for the challenge of battle. That the growth of his commitment to the hero's way entails a growth in his powers of perception—in the wisdom, which, the Musicians warn, "must live a bitter life" (264)—is underscored by Cuchulain's failure either to recognize the well when he comes upon it or to appreciate the difficulty of capturing its water:

Young Man.   . . . You can, it may be,
    Lead me to what I seek, a well wherein
    Three hazels drop their nuts and withered leaves,
    And where a solitary girl keeps watch

---

[38] Bradford, *Yeats at Work*, pp. 180 and 188.

Among grey boulders. He who drinks, they say,
Of that miraculous water lives for ever.
Old Man. And are there not before your eyes at the instant
Grey boulders and a solitary girl
And three stripped hazels?
Young Man.   But there is no well.
Old Man. Can you see nothing yonder?
Young Man.   I but see
A hollow among stones half-full of leaves.
Old Man. And do you think so great a gift is found
By no more toil than spreading out a sail,
And climbing a steep hill? O, folly of youth,
Why should that hollow place fill up for you,
That will not fill for me? . . .

                                                   (97–112)

At the Hawk's Well thus dramatizes a process of enlightenment. Though neither the Old Man nor Cuchulain desires from
the well anything but immortality, Yeats would have his audience, initiates in the traditions of Celtic lore, perceive in it, by
the hazels dropping nuts in its water, a source of that wisdom
which, with whatever bitterness, apotheosizes the hero into
myth. As the Old Man admonishes his visitor, physical prowess
alone—the strength to spread a sail and climb a hill—is insuffi-
cient.

For the Old Man has, despite his own myopia, achieved partial wisdom. He too lives a bitter life. He embodies intellect;[39]
and it is intellect, questioning the intuitive being, forcing him
to order and interpret impressions, that guides Cuchulain to the
well. That the Old Man, the faculties he bespeaks, are integral
to the hero's discovery of his vocation is implied not only by the
catechistic form their exchange takes but also by the prosodic
interlocking of their speeches, the Young Man's answers ex-

[39] See Ellmann, *The Man and the Masks*, p. 215. But Ellmann argues that
the intellect the Old Man embodies is specifically Yeats's, which strikes me as
an unrewarding and reductive construction to put on the play. Skene, *Cuchulain Plays*, p. 142, comes, I think, closer to Yeats's design, describing the Old
Man as a guide and interpreter for Cuchulain as he undergoes his spritual experience.

tending to their regular pentameter length the Old Man's interrogative lines.

Yet intellect, as the state of the Old Man and the landscape denote, is ultimately barren: it desires the wrong kind of immortality. The dancers have not, as the Old Man thinks, stolen his life. Having imposed on himself a passivity strikingly like the paralysis of Vladmir and Estragon in *Godot*, he has wasted it. In resisting the temptation to this passivity Cuchulain must leave intellect behind. Drawn from the well by the Guardian, he goes out, the stage-directions specify, *"as if in a dream."* "The Madness," in the words of the First Musician, "has laid hold upon him now" (216).

Madness does not, however, impair his ability to perceive. As Vendler observes, the First Musician's narration—"He has heard the plash;/ Look, he has turned his head" (222–23)—suggests that Cuchulain is aware of the water.[40] What he lacks is the will to act on his awareness. The Guardian's mesmeric eyes, her seductive dance have translated him into reverie. Which is to say that his subconscious has taken over; and his subconscious, given the alternatives of perishing "Among the desolate places" (253) or living "among indolent meadows" (263), makes the choice consistent, by the standards of reason, the bourgeois norms of society, with madness. As the practical (worldly) voice closing the Musicians' final song asks, " 'Who but an idiot would praise/ Dry stones in a well?' " (271–72). " 'Who but an idiot would praise/ A withered tree?' " (279–80).

The rightness of choosing idiocy is also established by the Musicians—who, while speaking for the figures in the play, speak too for the mind projecting the play—lamenting that Cuchulain pursuing the Guardian "has lost what may not be found/ Till men heap his burial-mound/ And all the history ends" (224–26). Personal immortality is inaccessible to beings caught in time. That the well holds the power to confer eternal life is mere rumor, as even Cuchulain acknowledges: "He who drinks, they say,/ Of that miraculous water lives for ever" (101–102). The Old Man, having spent his life beside the well,

[40] *Yeats's VISION and the Later Plays*, p. 212.

enters shivering with cold, indicative, like the bitter chill numbing the Beadsman's fingers in Keats's *Eve of St. Agnes*, of his approaching end. And his shivering contrasts with the shivering of the Guardian, as the "horrible deathless body" (214) slides through her veins. Though Cuchulain vows to her that, "Do what you will, I shall not leave this place/ Till I have grown immortal like yourself" (211–12), he is easily led from the well when the water plashes.

Yet he is once more right, if not as he thinks.[41] His subconscious, again, perceives better than his conscious, rational faculties. He is to grow immortal like the Guardian, turning from the water to pursue her, then to challenge Aoife, and to seek what adventures lie beyond, emerging as the hero of the ancient folk epic, *Táin Bó Cailnge*, its literary offshoots, and finally, in confrontation with the Guardian, this play. And Yeats would have us see Cuchulain's course as, at the crucial moment, consciously chosen. Asserting his intention to fight Aoife and her warriors, he departs, the stage-directions tell us, "*no longer as if in a dream.*"

Cuchulain has awakened not only from the reverie induced by the Hawk Woman but also from one version of *Ille*'s common dream, the immortality sought by the Old Man, to the threat, foreshadowed in the pallor of his ivory face, of dissipation and despair. Striking out after Aoife, he triggers the chain of events to culminate in the slaying of his son.

If he is tormented for taking the heroic path, he is, unlike the Old Man in his passivity, also rewarded. As Yeats implies through his arrangement of the dramas centering on Cuchulain in *Collected Plays*, the hero of *At the Hawk's Well* has embarked on creating his own myth. Though *At the Hawk's Well* was, if we except *Deirdre*, the third piece in the cycle to be written, it is the first to appear in *Collected Plays*. For, on the choice Cuchulain makes between the wandering heart and the heart at rest depends everything else: his triumph in the contest over the Green Helmet; the tragic circumstances leading to his fight

---

[41] As Sharoni, "Yeats's Unresolved Conflict," p. 155, perceptively observes, Cuchulain, by accepting the challenge, insures his immortality even while apparently repudiating the goal of his quest.

with the sea; his temptation by Fand; his last battle against Maeve's army, and his death, when weakened by six mortal wounds, at the hands of the Blind Man. In creating the myth encompassing these events he gains an immortality the Old Man can never know. Unlike the Old Man, who has merely his generic identity, Cuchulain proclaims his name and lineage at beginning and end: "He comes! Cuchulain, son of Sualtim, comes!" (249).[42]

In an epigram, defending his habit—disturbing to many of his friends—of subjecting his verse to incessant revision, Yeats concludes: "*It is myself that I remake.*" With each adventure —which is to say each play—Cuchulain too remakes himself. The disciplines of hero and poet, of action and contemplation, merge. Creating myth by becoming myth, Cuchulain enacts a paradigm of unity of being.

He epitomizes what Frank Kermode, focusing his argument on Yeats, particularly "In Memory of Major Robert Gregory," labels the Romantic Image. Defining the Image, Kermode stresses that it lacks "simple intellectual content, bearing the same relationship to thought as the dancer bears to the dance. As in dance, there is no disunity of being; 'the body is the soul.' "[43] The Guardian in what seems to the Old Man her stupidity prefigures that consummate instance of the Image in Yeatsian drama, The Queen in *The King of the Great Clock Tower*, whom the King—as uncomprehending as the Old Man— pronounces "Dumb as an image made of wood or metal" (25). Or, as Yeats sums it all up in the gnomic conclusion to "Among School Children," "How can we know the dancer from the dance?"

Like the Gregory of Yeats's elegy, like Yeats himself in "Among School Children," Cuchulain is thus image maker and image. "I am," intones the surrogate voice of the hero in the Musicians' final song, "but a mouthful of sweet air" (259). He understands himself, that is, to be an outgrowth of the breeze

---

[42] Moore, *Masks of Love and Death*, p. 204, aptly observes of the Old Man that, having been called but not chosen, he is cursed with a living death and refused the comfort of a name to live after him.

[43] *Romantic Image* (New York: Macmillan, 1957), pp. 43 and 48.

blowing him to the well, and symbolizing poetic inspiration; sweet because, to use the term Wordsworth or Coleridge might have used, and Yeats was to appropriate for the beautiful young man in *The Wanderings of Oisin*, the creative process is joyful as well as bitter. Cuchulain is, as the Musicians' song has it, "content to perish" (258) because he is free, unlike the Old Man, of material needs—"Folly alone I cherish,/ I choose it for my share" (255–56)—even of material existence.

Arriving at the well, he is greeted by the Old Man's alarmed question: "Who comes so suddenly into this place/ Where nothing thrives?" (80–81). For the Old Man, mired in a wasteland, seeking a goal not only beyond attainment but unworthy of attainment, nothing can thrive. For Cuchulain, who, out of that nothing fashions a new self, nothing thrives indeed. He is engaged in an activity, Romantic criticism, with which Yeats had more than passing acquaintance, has conventionally attributed to the poet poetizing: creation from nothing. And in this sense his pursuit of the Guardian is an allegory, in the tradition of *La Belle Dame Sans Merci*, of the poet's quest for his Muse. When *Hic* in "Ego Dominus Tuus" recalls Keats's "deliberate happiness," *Ille* replies: "I see a schoolboy when I think of him,/ With face and nose pressed to a sweet-shop window" (53, 55–56). Having provoked the Guardian to "rouse up the fierce women of the hills," Cuchulain is warned by the Old Man that "never till you are lying in the earth/ Can you know rest" (242, 244–45). True victory he is to learn—as, *Ille* argues, the tragic artist learns—is impossible to achieve in the mortal (fallen) world. Though Cuchulain may enjoy moments of triumph— Aoife will share his bed and bear his child—his ultimate destiny is the curse of Fand's unmoistened eyes. That this curse entails not only killing his son but also pursuing Fand herself Yeats dramatically asserts in *The Only Jealousy of Emer*, where Cuchulain, tempted almost to death by his demon lover, awakens to find himself afraid.

VI

Between Two Worlds

Glossing *The Only Jealousy of Emer* in *Four Plays for Dancers* (1921), Yeats reveals that he has, "While writing these plays, intended for some fifty people in a drawing-room or studio, . . . so rejoiced in my freedom from the stupidity of an ordinary audience that I have filled 'The Only Jealousy of Emer' with those little known convictions about the nature and history of a woman's beauty, which Robartes found in the *Speculum* of Gyraldus and in Arabia Deserta among the Judwalis." His disclosure looks forward, as his esoteric "sources" indicate, to *A Vision* (or what he coyly labels "my edition of the Robartes papers") still four years in the future. "The soul," he goes on, "through each cycle of its development is held to incarnate through twenty-eight typical incarnations, corresponding to the phases of the moon, the light part of the moon's disc symbolizing the subjective and the dark part . . . the objective nature, the wholly dark moon (called Phase 1) and the wholly light (called Phase 15) symbolizing complete objectivity and complete subjectivity respectively."[1] These convictions about woman's beauty, incarnate in *The Only Jealousy of Emer* largely in Fand, also look back to the various embodiments of *La Belle Dame San Merci* haunting Yeats's early verse: pearl-pale Niamh in *The Wanderings of Oisin*; Dectora covering Forgael with her hair in *The Shadowy Waters*; the glimmering girl in "The Song of the Wandering Aengus"; in general the figure Allen R. Grossman, in his incisive study of *The Wind Among the Reeds*, dubs "the white woman."[2]

That the white woman, even in her initial appearances, came to Yeats radiating a lunar sheen is manifest from any number of her antecedents in the nineteenth century, among them the temptress of Flaubert's Saint Anthony, of whom Yeats read in

[1] *Variorum Plays*, p. 566.

[2] *Poetic Knowledge in the Early Yeats* (Charlottesville: The University Press of Virginia, 1969). See especially p. 21, where Grossman outlines the characteristics of the Yeatsian white woman.

Lafcadio Hearne's translation of 1895, where he found her portrayed as "really . . . the moon."[3] That she confronts Cuchulain in the person of Fand is suggested by the question he asks as she circles him in her dance: "Who is it stands before me there/ Shedding such light from limb and hair/ As when the moon, complete at last/ With every labouring crescent past,/ And lonely with extreme delight,/ Flings out upon the fifteenth night?" (220–25). Cuchulain's perception of the moon flinging itself before his mind's eye reflects the impact of Fand's dance upon him, and recalls both the First Musician's white frail bird "thrown/ Between dark furrows upon the ploughed land" (5–6) and, among the bird's human corollaries, Emer herself claiming to be "thrown beyond" (171) the power of Bricriu. Fand's beauty, however, Cuchulain sees as self-generated, while the beauty of the bird is passive, subject to a force beyond its control, and Emer must submit to Bricriu to restore her husband.

Cuchulain discerns in Fand the finished artifact, the Image materialized. And her state of being as seemingly a gold, bronze, brass, or silver idol; her phase, "the invisible fifteenth incarnation," described by Yeats's Note on *The Only Jealousy of Emer* in *Four Plays for Dancers* as "that of the greatest possible bodily beauty,"[4] encourage him in this belief. Lured by Fand, Cuchulain has been translated into vision: he has entered the depths of the mind, the *Anima Mundi*, which is why Bricriu must give Emer sight before she can penetrate the dark dividing her from him.

Cuchulain thus perceives Fand as living a kind of Edenic existence, beyond all "labouring" crescents. Yeats's use of "labour" to describe the condition Fand has escaped echoes its crucial use much earlier in "Adam's Curse," where "that beautiful mild woman" observes: " 'To be born woman is to know—/ Although they do not talk of it at school—/ That we must labour to be beautiful' " (18–20). Labor sums up the curse Adam has visited upon the world; for labor—as the pangs of childbirth, the stitching and unstitching of the poet's line, the

[3] *The Temptation of Saint Anthony* (London: M.S. Nichols, 1895), p. 271. Quoted in Grossman, *Poetic Knowledge*, p. 22.

[4] *Variorum Plays*, p. 566.

preparation of a woman's face—comprises man's struggle against the erosive effects of time, imaged in "Adam's Curse," as in *The Only Jealousy of Emer*, not only by the moon but also by a shell tossed upon the sand: "We sat grown quiet at the name of love;/ We saw the last embers of daylight die,/ And in the trembling blue-green of the sky/ A moon, worn as if it had been a shell/ Washed by time's waters as they rose and fell/ About the stars and broke in days and years" (28–33).

The shell in the First Musician's song constitutes the final stage in a transformation, initially turning mortal beauty from its physical form as a woman into metaphor, the white sea-bird. Transformation is itself a paradigm of change; and posing the bird between ploughed furrows links it to one aspect of the labor man must endure to cope with a world of change.[5] In contrast to the metallic figure of Fand the bird is organic: like the shell caught by the power of the storm, "fragile, exquisite, pale" (16). The shell is, moreover, the husk of a dead creature, comparable to the body on the fisher's pallet, of whom Eithne Inguba asks, "is he dead?" (56). Only Emer's faith in Cuchulain's greatness keeps her from concluding that he is: "Although they have dressed him out in his grave-clothes/ And stretched his limbs, Cuchulain is not dead;/ The very heavens when that day's at hand,/ So that his death may not lack ceremony,/ Will throw out fires, and the earth grow red with blood./ There shall not be a scullion but foreknows it/ Like the world's end" (57–63).

In *Fighting the Waves*, his prose rewriting of *The Only Jealousy of Emer*, Yeats drastically abridges this speech, replacing the indefinite "they" with the specific attribution that "The fishermen think him dead" (58), and deleting the promise of cosmic portents to accompany Cuchulain's passing. Yeats rewrote the play, he explains, introducing its prose version in *Wheels and Butterflies*, "not only to fit it for [the public stage]

---

[5] Nathan, *Tragic Drama*, p. 232, proposes an analogous reading of the "ploughed land" as indicative of human purpose set against the inhuman force of the sea. And Skene, *Cuchulain Plays*, p. 204, suggests that Cuchulain's description of the crescents preceding Fand's as "labouring" is meant by Yeats to recall the ploughed land of the opening song.

but to free it from abstraction and confusion"; by which he means simplifying its language and leaving, as he puts it, "imaginative suggestion to dancers, singers, musicians."[6] In this effort he excises the verbal duet of Cuchulain and Fand, reducing the play to a struggle between man and daimon—a conflict central, as Nathan urges, to Yeats's drama overall but in *The Only Jealousy of Emer*, I think, symbolic of something more.

The producer railing at the vileness of the age in the prologue to *The Death of Cuchulain* insists on an audience knowing "the old epics and Mr. Yeats' plays about them," adding that "such people, however poor, have libraries of their own" (s–u). *Fighting the Waves* is a concession to the vileness of the age, assuming an audience without special knowledge, written for the sciolists "educating themselves out of the Book Societies" (v–w).

This narrowing of Yeats's focus, his relaxation of the demands he conventionally makes on an audience, is mirrored by the shift in the play's title. While *Fighting the Waves* obviously evokes Cuchulain battling the sea at the climax of *On Baile's Strand*, the episode leading to his temptation by Fand, it also defines the challenge faced by Emer and (with whatever reluctance) Eithne Inguba: "We are," says Emer, in both versions of the scenario, "two women struggling with the sea" (*FW*, 140–42; *OJE*, 123).

Her assertion, with the dialogue of Cuchulain and Fand eliminated, provides a nearly adequate statement of the play's dramatic conflict. In rewriting *The Only Jealousy of Emer* as *Fighting the Waves* Yeats has cut the symbolic heart from his artifact, sacrificing vision to its vitality as a theatrical event. (Which is why it is *The Only Jealousy of Emer* that he chooses to preserve in *Collected Plays*.) "Fighting the Waves," as Yeats allows, if somewhat exaggeratedly, in his Introduction, "is in itself nothing, a mere occasion for sculptor and dancer, for the exciting dramatic music of George Antheil."[7]

For the symbolic heart of Yeats's construct lies in the dialogue of Cuchulain and Fand, and especially in Fand's apparent promise to free Cuchulain of his entrapment in time. De-

---

[6] *Variorum Plays*, p. 567.   [7] *Ibid.*, p. 567.

parting from the archetype of the hero as Irish Achilles, which he found in Lady Gregory and her forebears, Yeats renders Cuchulain an aging figure. Mocked by Fand for having lost the ardor energizing his pursuit of her at the hawk's well, Cuchulain admits that he is no longer "The young and passionate man I was" (250). He confronts her, indeed, in the posture of the Old Man, bent double like the thorn trees, keeping his vain watch on the accursed mountain. "What," Fand asks him, "pulled your hands about your feet,/ Pulled down your head upon your knees,/ And hid your face?" (227–29). His answer, "Old memories" (229), subsumes not only time but the whole of his human experience: "A woman in her happy youth/ Before her man had broken troth,/ Dead men and women" (231–32). It is from the burden of that experience, with its moral consequences, that Fand seems to offer release:

> *Woman of the Sidhe*. Then kiss my mouth. Though memory
>   Be beauty's bitterest enemy
>   I have no dread, for at my kiss
>   Memory on the moment vanishes;
>   Nothing but beauty can remain.
> *Ghost of Cuchulain*. And shall I never know again
>   Intricacies of blind remorse?
> *Woman of the Sidhe*. Time shall seem to stay his course;
>   When your mouth and my mouth meet
>   All my round shall be complete
>   Imagining all its circles run;
>   And there shall be oblivion
>   Even to quench Cuchulain's drouth,
>   Even to still that heart.
>
>   (254–67)

As Wilson pointed out long ago, Fand's invitation threatens Cuchulain with the fatal touch of the *Sidhe*, the "Kiss of Death."[8] Proposed as a nostrum for quenching even his drought, it—"oblivion"—constitutes the real substance of the water plashing in the Well of Immortality. The operative word

---

[8] *Yeats's Iconography*, pp. 75 and 111. See also Vendler, *Yeats's VISION*, p. 224.

in Fand's appeal is "seem." *The Only Jealousy of Emer* repeats the statement, implicit in *At the Hawk's Well*, that eternal life lies beyond the grasp of the most extraordinary human being. A son of Lugh, Cuchulain is partly of the gods: "what," asks Fand, "could make you fit to wive/ With flesh and blood, being born to live/ Where no one speaks of broken troth . . . ?" (280–82).

The question is rhetorical, expressing her vexation at discovering Emer—above whom, as Fand reminds him, Cuchulain has valued every slut or loose-tongued schemer catching his eye—between her and the hero's kiss. "So then it is she," Fand exclaims, "made you impure with memory" (268–69). Yeats, behind Fand, is using "impure" with deliberate irony. In the view of the world Cuchulain is made impure by his adulteries, his renunciation of Emer's claim upon him. And a part of him acquiesces in this judgment, his memory calling to his mind's eye a past of domestic contentment disrupted by his transgressions: "O Emer, Emer, there we stand;/ Side by side and hand in hand/ Tread the threshold of the house/ As when our parents married us" (270–73). In the view of the *Sidhe* he is made impure by his inability to renounce Emer altogether, to purge himself of memory. For Fand, his impurity resides in his mortal state, the imperfections to which he is heir by having been born into the world.

Cuchulain is posed with an insoluble dilemma: as a man of heroic appetite, he cannot live at his ease among the comforts Emer bespeaks; as a man, he cannot possess Fand. Yeats is rewriting *La Belle Dame Sans Merci*. When the knight-at-arms (in Keats's original version) tries to love the faery lady physically, shutting "her wild wild eyes/ With kisses four," she lulls him asleep and disappears, because, not being physical, she cannot be loved physically. When Cuchulain yearns for Fand's mouth, he is thwarted by Emer, debris from his earthly life. For both heroes, the reward of the quest is frustration, debility. In his sleep the knight sees "pale kings and princes too,/ Pale warriors, death-pale were they all," reflections of himself "palely loitering" on the cold hill's side. In the reverie induced by the dance of the Guardian on another cold hill's side Cuchulain "grows pale and staggers to his feet" (217), fulfilling the doom presaged in the pallor of the ivory face he wears on his climb to the well. What the figures in his dream tell the knight is that " 'La Belle Dame sans Merci/ Hath thee in thrall!' " And thrall-dom is the fate of those lured by the *Sidhe*. As Emer, seemingly echoing the ritual song of the Women in *On Baile's Strand*, says of Fand: "I know her sort./ They find our men asleep, weary with war,/ Lap them in cloudy hair or kiss their lips;/ Our men awake in ignorance of it all,/ But when we take them in our arms at night/ We cannot break their solitude" (212–17).

Or, as Bricriu warns Emer, "the Sidhe/ Are dextrous fishers and they fish for men/ With dreams upon the hook" (204–206). They are ironically like Christ, who was also a dextrous fisher of men, and who for Yeats, as *Calvary* (written immediately after *The Only Jealousy of Emer*) avers, baited his hook with dreams. Each promises to man an immortality he cannot produce.

Fishing (of which Yeats was himself fond) serves him as a recurrent image of the quest for a timeless paradise and the beauty it holds. In "The Song of the Wandering Aengus" (some twenty years before *The Only Jealousy of Emer*) he had, while reversing the roles of fish and fisher, shaped this image to the same end:

> I went out to the hazel wood,
> Because a fire was in my head,
> And cut and peeled a hazel wand,
> And hooked a berry to a thread;
> And when white moths were on the wing,
> And moth-like stars were flickering out,
> I dropped a berry in a stream,
> And caught a little silver trout.
>
> (1–8)

The transformation of the trout into a glimmering girl marks her as of the same magical realm as Fand, who has "dreamed herself into that shape [Emer calls it 'a lie' (208)] that [Cuchulain]/ May glitter in her basket" (203–204). The consequence of this encounter with Fand is akin to the consequence of

Aengus's encounter with his temptress or of the knight's with
La Belle Dame. Like Aengus grown old with futile wandering
or the knight left haggard, woe-begone, Cuchulain wakes
shaken by fear.

He turns in his distress to Eithne Inguba because she—as
mistress rather than wife, a woman outside society's constrict-
ing domestic arrangements—appears to him closer than Emer
to the ideal embodied by Fand. Cuchulain is, as Fand perceives
him, unfit for marriage with flesh and blood because born to
live where "all have washed out of their eyes/ Windblown dirt
of their memories/ To improve their sight" (283–85). He seems
meant for the kind of world Niamh, in words almost precisely
anticipating Fand's to Cuchulain, offers Oisin: "Where men
have heaped no burial mounds,/ And the days pass by like a
wayward tune,/ Where broken faith has never been known/ And
the blushes of first love never have flown" (I, 82–85). That
Cuchulain detects some faint echo of this world and of Fand
tempting him to it in Eithne Inguba is suggested by his cry to
Eithne on waking, "your arms, your arms!" (303), paralleling
his earlier cry to Fand, "Your mouth, your mouth!" (285).

But Cuchulain is duped, both by the presence of Eithne, who
has not, despite her claim, "won him from the sea" (301), and
the promise of Fand, whose world too is subject to time. As
Emer, detecting the subterfuge even before Bricriu arises to
give her sight, speculates of the body on the fisherman's bed,
"It may be/ An image has been put into his likeness,/ Or some
stark horseman grown too old to ride/ Among the troops of
Manannan . . ./ Now that his joints are stiff" (85–90). Bricriu,
his arm withered to the bone, confronts her not merely with the
truth of her conjecture but with the larger truth that the *Sidhe*
also age and decay.

Observing that Fand, in a scene Yeats was eventually to ex-
cise, addresses Bricriu as "you that have no living light, but
dropped from a last leprous crescent of the moon" (288 ee–ff),
Vendler argues that the real conflict lies between them, deform-
ity undermining aesthetic perfection.[9] This seems to me a co-
gent reading of Yeats's allegory, except that Fand is herself, as

[9] *Yeats's VISION and the Later Plays*, p. 221.

she concedes, imperfect. When Cuchulain asks who stands before him, she replies, evading rather than answering his question: "Because I long I am not complete" (226). Until he kisses her, completing her round, she can have no final identity.

The duet of Cuchulain and Fand, then, dramatizes the dependence of the Muse on her poet. Without a commitment reaching even to the obliteration of the artist's self, she cannot (moonlike) realize her fullness, emerging as the finished artifact, that gold, bronze, brass, or silver idol freed from the effects of mutability. His failures are her defeats. And since he can succeed alone through death, defeat is her recurrent lot. Niamh spirits Oisin away to the Island of the Living only to have a warrior's broken lance remind him "how the Fenians stept/ Along the blood-bedabbled plains,/ Equal to good or grievous chance" (I, 370–72). She pits him against a shape-changing demon, Mutability itself, only to have it rise from the sea every four days until a beech-bough drifts ashore to remind Oisin "how I had stood by white-haired Finn/ Under a beech an Almhuin and heard the thin/ Outcry of bats" (II, 227–29). She induces him to the sleep of forgetfulness only to have a falling starling remind him of the birds that "foregathered 'neath a moon waking white as a shell/ When the Fenians made foray at morning with Bran, Sceolan, Lomair" (III, 103–104).

Oisin's wanderings describe a series of circles, each closed by the discovery that he, like Cuchulain, has been rendered impure with memory or, as Niamh laments to him, that "there moves alive in your fingers the fluttering sadness of earth" (III, 124). Fand too must presumably learn that there moves alive in Cuchulain's fingers the fluttering sadness of earth, and that to take a lover pulsing with such sadness means frustration for her as for him. In the play's original version, indeed, Cuchulain lectures her on the human condition:

> I know you now in all your ignorance
> Of all whereby a lover's quiet is rent.
> What dread so great as that he should forget
> The least chance sight or sound, or scratch or mark
> On an old door, or frail bird heard or seen

In the incredible light love cast
All round about her some forlorn lost day?

                                        (288 g–m)

His message is the message of the lovers in *Deirdre* or of Edain
in *The Two Kings*: that the anguish of love, the prospect of
loss—the very precariousness to life the *Sidhe* escape—are what
infuse human experience with tragic meaning. "How could you
know/ That man is held to those whom he has loved/ By pain
they give, or pain that he has given—/ Intricacies of pain" (288
y–bb). Unlike Niamh—who, asked by Oisin which of her is-
lands is the Island of Content, must weeping confess, "None
know" (II, 249)—Fand remains insulated, however, from
Cuchulain's dilemma, sending him off to demand his life of
Manannan, adopting the stance of beautiful woman spurned: "I
am ashamed/ That being of the deathless shades I chose/ A man
so knotted to impurity" (288 bb–dd).

Fand's proposal that Cuchulain seek recovery of his mortal
life from Manannan—that, as she puts it, having failed to
forget in a god's fashion, he may "now . . . forget in a man's"
(288 r)—echoes the play's sources, not only Lady Gregory's
Cuchulain of Muirthemne but Blunt's *Fand*. Yeats finally dis-
cards this echo, muting the whole exchange between his Cuchulain and Fand, as well as the quarrel between Bricriu and Fand
to follow, because he would not have her seen as the petulant
mistress thwarted by a patient Griselda of a wife. He wishes instead to stress the all but unbridgeable gap between Emer's
world and Fand's, the impossibility of crossing the line, as Fand
tempts Cuchulain to do, yet retaining human consciousness.
Meeting the remnant of the Fianna, their memories weighted
with thoughts of the slaughter "On Gabhra's raven covered
plain" (I, 43), Niamh asks why they wind no horn "And every
hero droop his head . . . The hunting of heroes should be glad"
(I, 32–39). Oisin himself, mounted on Niamh's horse, wrapped
in her arms, ignores the pleas of his comrades, and rides out
with her "from the human lands" (I, 114). Fand contemplates
memory, though beauty's bitterest enemy, without dread,
while Cuchulain wakes, crying to Eithne Inguba that "I have
been in some strange place and am afraid" (304).

Unencumbered by intricacies of pain or remorse, Fand has no experience that would enable her to appreciate the tensions encumbering Cuchulain. Tangled in such intricacies by his very nature, Cuchulain has no resources that would enable him to embrace Fand, except at the cost of his physical being. Fand is herself, as Bricriu admonishes Emer when she draws her knife, but a dream, a "body of air" (218). That the suffering wife should come between her husband and his demon lover, at the last instant preventing their union, is thus almost inevitable. He is wedded to her, and to the mortality she embodies.

When Bricriu presses Emer to renounce Cuchulain, urging that "There is still time. . . . There is still a moment left" (290–94), he means not only that she can yet save Cuchulain from Fand by relinquishing him herself but also that time continues to exist for him, despite his apparent passage into the *Sidhe*. And time exists for Fand too. Opening her campaign of seduction, she asks: "Could you that have loved many a woman/ That did not reach beyond the human,/ Lacking a day to be complete,/ Love one that, though her heart can beat,/ Lacks it but by an hour or so?" (234–38). Wilson cites this question in arguing that each of the characters in *The Only Jealousy of Emer* enacts a specific phase of Yeats's system: as Fand, the approximation of perfect beauty, lacking completeness but by an hour, occupies Phase 15, Eithne Inguba, a day shy of completeness, belongs to Phase 14, one of two phases in which "the greatest human beauty becomes possible."[10] Syntactically, however, "lacking a day to be complete" may describe Cuchulain as well as Eithne. Both are, in contrast to Fand, firmly rooted in the mundane world. Though Wilson reasonably assigns Cuchulain to Phase 12, Nietzsche's phase, the hero's, the dramatic complexity of the play—which is something apart from the allegorical rigor of Yeats's design in *A Vision*—favors Vendler's view that only Fand approaches the singularity of a "pure" incarnation.[11]

And even Fand falls short. Her encounter with Cuchulain,

[10] *Yeats's Iconography*, pp. 107 and 109. The description of Phase 14 is quoted from *A Vision* (New York: Macmillan, 1961), p. 131.

[11] See *Yeats's Iconography*, p. 108, and *Yeats's VISION and the Later Plays*, p. 217.

like Niamh's attempts to empty Oisin's heart of its mortal dream, comprises one in a series of cycles, implied by the lunar scheme charting her progress toward perfection. Anticipating the apotheosis to be brought about by Cuchulain's kiss, she foresees her round "imagining" itself complete. To imagine something happening is, in a psychic world, to make it happen. But it is also to suggest, especially conjoined to Fand's claim of time seeming stayed, that what happens is an appearance, to evaporate when the force of imagination is removed. The dance of Cuchulain and Fand, like the seduction of the knight by *La Belle Dame*, symbolizes a recurrent striving toward union, never in this life to be consummated.

Which is why the process of calling Cuchulain back begins with Eithne Inguba's altogether fleshly kiss, why the *Sidhe* are said to fish for men with dreams upon the hook, and why the setting of *The Only Jealousy of Emer* is "a poor fisher's house" (33). Emer too is fishing for a man, first with Eithne Inguba upon the hook, then with her own dream "that some day somewhere/ We'll sit together at the hearth again" (103–104). Yeats has framed his crucial episode, with the setting around Emer at beginning and end posed against the dramatization of Bricriu's image of Fand as fisher, thereby stressing the gap between the apparently perfectible realm of the *Sidhe*, the imagination, and the irretrievably flawed world of men. The trappings identifying the house as a poor fisher's—the net, the long oar—are tools man has invented to cope with his need to labor, Adam's curse. That curse is manifest in the sacrifice Emer must make to save Cuchulain. As Bricriu explains, in answering her question, "Do the Sidhe bargain?" (158): "When they would free a captive/ They take in ransom a less valued thing./ The fisher, when some knowledgeable man/ restores to him his wife, or son, or daughter,/ Knows he must lose a boat or net, or it may be/ The cow that gives his children milk; and some/ Have offered their own lives" (158–64).

Sacrifice, the imperfect fulfillment, if not complete frustration, of desire, sums up the human condition. Bricriu, discord, what Yeats terms elsewhere "The wrong of unshapely things," defines the state against which fallen man, and especially artist-man, is doomed through time to struggle. "How many centuries," asks the First Musician in the opening song, "spent the sedentary soul/ In toils of measurement/ Beyond eagle or mole,/ Beyond hearing or seeing,/ Or Archimedes' guess,/ To raise into being/ That loveliness?" (7–14). The grammatical inversion apprehends one of Yeats's nicest ambiguities, anticipating those extraordinary lines, "A mouth that has no moisture and no breath/ Breathless mouths may summon," from "Byzantium." If, as Skene reads the Musician's song, the soul, the collective artistic consciousness, spends centuries building toward the loveliness of art, the realized Image, those centuries also spend—drain—the toiling soul.[12] That loveliness raised into being amid its creator's dissipation and despair looks both back to the figure of the bird, wrought to simulate a woman's beauty and thrown precariously upon the ploughed land, and forward to the metallic Fand, brought to within an hour of becoming an artifice of eternity.

The first Musician's question informs the symbolism of the play: reflecting the odds with which the artist must contend; conceding that, restricted by his more or less three score years and ten, he must almost inevitably fail. That he perseveres in the face of failure—finding his mask in disappointment as the hero in defeat—elevates him to a stature akin, the Musician suggests in his second sequence of questions, to Cuchulain's own: "What death/ what discipline?/ What bonds no man could unbind,/ Being imagined within/ The labyrinth of the mind,/ What pursuing or fleeing,/ What wounds, what bloody press,/ Dragged into being/ This loveliness?" (21–28). Myths, whether made by hero or artist, unfold by analogous processes, involving not only the disciplined control of mathematical inquiry but also immersion in the destructive element; projecting their makers beyond the borders of physical space, the limits implied by soaring eagle and burrowing mole, into the *Anima Mundi*, the deeps of the mind itself.

This confrontation with violence and death, with life lived at the outer edges of possibility, is, as Yeats found confirmed in the work of Synge, whose *Riders to the Sea* seems to underlie

[12] For Skene's reading, see *Cuchulain Plays*, p. 202.

the setting for *The Only Jealousy of Emer*, what renders heroic and artistic experience comparable. Memorializing his friend in 1910, Yeats claims for Synge's portrayals of the peasantry on Inishman and the Blaskets that "Here were men and women who under the weight of their necessity lived, as the artist lives, in the presence of death and childhood, and the great affections and the orgiastic moment when life outleaps its limits, and who, as it is always with those who have refused or escaped the trivial and temporary, had dignity and good manners where manners mattered."[13]

They lived as the struggling women and their prize in *The Only Jealousy of Emer*, of whom Yeats wrote to Olivia Shakespear in 1929, after the play was finally performed at the Abbey: "I felt that the sea was eternity and that they were all upon its edge."[14] He might have been characterizing the state of Maurya, her two daughters, and last son in *Riders to the Sea*, even to the storm which, as it throws the bird onto the land, emphasizing the helplessness of frail creatures before its brute power, bursts through the door of Maurya's cottage, emphasizing man's helplessness before the cruelty of blind nature.

While Yeats absorbs elements from Synge's drama, however, he refashions them to his own ends. Wilson reads his remark to Olivia Shakespear (I think rightly) as suggesting a correspondence between the sea and the *Anima Mundi*.[15] The storm throwing the bird or, in its transformed guise, the shell onto the land marks one of several Yeatsian variants on the traditional Romantic metaphor of wind as inspiration conjuring images from the deeps of the mind. And that storm also throws Cuchulain onto the land. As Emer tells Eithne Inguba, "the waves washed his senseless image up/ And laid it at this door" (82–83).

The setting for *The Only Jealousy of Emer* thus repeats the settings for *The Green Helmet*, *On Baile's Strand*, and *The Land of Heart's Desire*, with the actions of all four plays unfolding against interior backdrops, their doors to the outside sym-

13 "J. M. Synge and the Ireland of His Time," *Essays and Introductions*, p. 325.
14 Wade, *Letters*, p. 768.   15 *Yeats's Iconography*, p. 97.

bolizing the passage between the mundane world, its trappings of home and hearth, and the mystery beyond.[16] That Yeats would have his audience take this meaning from the scene he establishes through the First Musician describing Eithne's entrance and hearing in the wash of waves upon the beach their rejection of her all too vulnerable beauty: "She stands a moment in the open door./ Beyond the open door the bitter sea,/ The shining, bitter sea, is crying out,/ [*singing*] White shell, white wing!/ I will not choose for my friend/ A frail, unserviceable thing/ That drifts and dreams, and but knows/ That waters are without end/ And that wind blows" (41–49).

The Musician's song imposes consciousness on what in Synge remains unconscious nature. Yeats is asserting the power of the imagination to alter reality, using his Musician, as in *At the Hawk's Well*, to guide the audience toward a proper understanding of the play. The sea's cry foreshadows Cuchulain's fate. He too turns out, for Fand's needs, frail and unserviceable. Her defeat by his mortality as well as Emer's love—which is to say both the weakness and the strength of the human condition—is crystallized in the central stanza of the Musicians' final song:

> Although the door be shut
> And all seem well enough,
> Although wide world hold not
> A man but will give you his love
> The moment he has looked at you,
> He that has loved the best
> May turn from a statue
> His too human breast.
>
> (318–25)

The song reflects the structure, and to some degree the strategy, of the play proper. Composed of three regular stanzas, each followed by a refrain, it encapsulates man's longing toward, yet loss of, *La Belle Dame*, always holding before the au-

[16] Wilson suggests the parallel between the symbolic situation in *The Green Helmet*, with the Red Man entering through a door open on the stormy sea, and that in *The Only Jealousy of Emer*. *Ibid.*, pp. 102–103.

dience the mortal state—"O bitter reward/ Of many a tragic tomb!"—that makes longing and loss inevitable. It moves, that is, from the temptation itself, Cuchulain's meeting with the statue, to its crisis, the conflict within him between the lure of Fand and the memory of Emer, to the realization that, even should Fand be fulfilled, the life for her lover, for the onlookers—Emer, the audience—can at best go on as it has: "When beauty is complete/ Your own thought will have died/ And danger not be diminished;/ Dimmed at three-quarter light,/ When the moon's round is finished/ The stars are out of sight" (333–38).

That knowledge, embedded in myth, is the bitter reward of many a tragic tomb. Bringing the audience to that knowledge, clarifying the myth, is what the play is shaped to do. Like *Deirdre* and *At the Hawk's Well*, or with less exactitude *On Baile's Strand* and *The Green Helmet*, its action emerges from the narrative of the First Musician calling before the audience's eyes the poor fisher's house. Yeats accents the role of the Musician as the teller of a story, as it were an old wives' tale, by having him employ the story-teller's rhetorical strategy. He accumulates details with a kind of systematic periodicity, building toward a moment of intense life involving agents of gigantic stature:

A man lies dead or swooning,
That amorous man,
That amorous, violent man, renowned Cuchulain,
Queen Emer at his side.

(34–37)

or:

. . . now one comes on hesitating feet,
Young Eithne Inguba, Cuchulain's mistress.

(39–40)

The audience is once more being made witness to the translation of word into image, the creative process itself. The scenario moves, roughly like its final song, from their world, epitomized by Emer and the fisher's house, into Fand's world of gold enameling, back to their world. That Fand's world consists in monuments of all but unaging intellect rather than fish, flesh, or fowl Yeats's shift from blank verse, suggesting normal speech, to octosyllabic couplets, their form calling attention to them as artifice, to blank verse again is meant to stress. That Cuchulain and Fand in their dance seem insulated from the vicissitudes of fish, flesh, or fowl the shut door of the song implies.[17] But the shut door is an illusion. Emer decides the drama taking place behind it simply by renouncing what she cannot regain anyway. As Bricriu ruthlessly insists to her, "He'll never sit beside you at the hearth/ Or make old bones, but die of wounds and toil/ On some far shore or mountain, a strange woman/ Beside his mattress" (180–83). Cuchulain is himself thrust back through the door into Eithne Inguba's arms. And the audience, given sight by Yeats as Emer by Bricriu, watches an encounter in Faery.

The audience, as in *At the Hawk's Well*, have revealed to them the deeps of the playwright's mind. When the Musicians ask, opening their final song, "Why does your heart beat thus?" (305), they are addressing both the participants in this drama, suspended before the mind's eye in their moment of passionate intensity, and the galleries, who also "have met in a man's house/ A statue of solitude,/ Moving there and walking" (307–309). Yeats forces them to confront not only their response to his vision as a staged event but, what is inherent in the beating heart, mortality—theirs, as well as Cuchulain's, Emer's, Eithne Inguba's, even perhaps Fand's and his own. He is using his Musicians, as he had in *Deirdre* and *At the Hawk's Well*, to engage the audience in his psychic world, in effect to make his consciousness theirs.

Yet he appears to have retreated from the faith behind the opening song of *At the Hawk's Well*: that the audience might actually participate in the creative process. The Musicians in *The Only Jealousy of Emer*, speaking in part for the audience, resign themselves to the passivity of mere spectators: "we

---

[17] Nathan, *Tragic Drama*, p. 230, reads Yeats's shift from blank verse to octosyllabic couplets as an effort to remove Cuchulain and Fand to a realm alien to Emer and Eithne Inguba.

though astonished are dumb/ Or give but a sigh and a word,/ A passing word" (315–17, 328–30, 341–43). Their resignation, essentially the substance of the refrain to the final song, is the note on which the play ends.

Yeats has restored what his introduction of Musicians and his departure from the proscenium stage had begun to break down, the distance between the playwright, his agents, and his audience. Despite the lively critical debate over Emer's claim, through her sacrifice, to heroic stature, hers is a play without a heroine in the technical sense. Each of the principals is, as the lunar scheme underlying Yeats's symbolism hints, caught in a pattern of behavior, which he may repeat but not break, keeping him from doing other than he does. And the audience is similarly caught. Confined to their seats while the drama unfolds before them, capable of no more response than a sigh and a passing word, they manifest a removal from the action, measuring the gap between their present and the mythic past of Emer and Cuchulain, at once blessed and cursed by its access, however temporary, to the supernatural. In the present the artist alone is comparably blessed and cursed, and then at immense psychic cost. He is as little of the world of his audience as they of the world of his artifact. He is instead, like those Irish Yeats invokes in "The Statues," "born into that ancient sect/ But thrown upon this filthy modern tide/ And by its formless spawning fury wrecked" (28–30).

Those Irish, among whom Yeats explicitly numbers himself ("We"), stand parallel to the boys and girls of the poem's first stanza, pressing "at midnight in some public place/ Live lips upon a plummet-measured face" (7–8)—essentially the consummation to which Fand has invited Cuchulain. Like the Musician's sedentary soul, the boys and girls are aroused by a loveliness rising from toils of measurement, what Blake and Yeats earlier in his career had condemned as Mathematic Form. But Yeats's mind has changed. The bonds Orc had burst, against which the Cuchulain of *On Baile's Strand* struggled, have come to seem an inevitable, if painful, adjunct to the artist's discipline: in "The Statues" the very lineaments to which he must hold to avoid drowning in the tide of Asiatic formlessness; in *The Only Jealousy of Emer*, among the necessary burdens enabling him to drag into being "This loveliness"—ultimately, the play itself.

Though "The Statues" and *The Only Jealousy of Emer* project the same values, even something of the same symbolism, the poem follows the play by over two decades. Dated April 9, 1938, "The Statues" reached completion as Yeats was gestating the last of the dramas in his heroic cycle, *The Death of Cuchulain*. Indeed, in posing the question, "When Pearse summoned Cuchulain to his side,/ What stalked through the Post Office?" (25–26), "The Statues" adumbrates the song with which *The Death of Cuchulain* and Yeats's dramatic career close. In both modes, lyric and dramatic, he re-engages the dilemma implicit in *The Only Jealousy of Emer*: how does the artist cope with a world in which he finds himself a man hopelessly out of phase? Yeats is about to cast his final cold eye on life, on death.

VII

A Mansion in Eternity

The Death of Cuchulain is Yeats's dramatic epitaph: written to acknowledge that time was running down for himself and the era in which he lived; that his long struggle as a man out of phase was reaching its tragic close, rendered futile by history, pushing the Christian dispensation toward collapse. Even the cycle, which this play presumably completes, Yeats is forced, or so it seems to him, to leave imperfect. He would, he reveals in his *Wheels and Butterflies* Introduction to *Fighting the Waves*, have tried not only the Death of Cuchulain but also the Battle of the Ford, "had not the mood of Ireland changed."

Thus, it may be, the twenty year lapse between *The Only Jealousy of Emer* and his next attempt at an original Cuchulain drama. The civilization that Phidias and his disciples preserved with mallet and chisel, that Yeats has also striven to preserve in the myth engendered by his poems and plays, appears finally to be succumbing to "Asiatic vague immensities." In a statement from his philosophical epitaph, *On the Boiler*, and singled out by Daniel Albright to gloss "The Statues," Yeats asserts: "There are moments when I am certain that art must once again accept those Greek proportions which carry into plastic art the Pythagorean numbers, those faces which are divine because all there is empty and measured. Europe was not born when Greek galleys defeated the Persian hordes at Salamis, but when the Doric studios sent out those broad-backed marble statues against the multiform, vague expressive Asiatic sea, they gave to the sexual instinct of Europe its goal, its fixed type."

That fixed type Yeats finds exemplified in the Swedish actress he recalls "standing upon some boat's edge between Portofino and Rapallo, or riding the foam upon a plank towed behind a speed-boat," and who in her statuesque sun-burned beauty suggests the gold, brass, bronze, or silver idol, Fand. In her Yeats recognizes "flesh-tints that Greek painters loved as have all the greatest since," giving the lie to "those red patches

130

whereby our democratic painters prove that they have really studied from the life."[1] Only the artist self-consciously upholding tradition stands between the world and chaos. And the influence of the artist has yielded, as Yeats observes in *Wheels and Butterflies*, to a positivistic science worshipped by the culture of "Garrets and Cellars."[2]

It is this awareness of the artist's growing futility, essentially of his own futility, which motivates the speech of the Old Man serving, instead of the usual Musicians' song, as prologue to *The Death of Cuchulain*. Vendler dismisses this prologue as "rant," arguing that Yeats would have excised it had he lived to revise the play.[3] Yet what the Old Man says hardly differs in tone from some of the more bitter fulminations in *On the Boiler*, and repeats the kind of pronouncements on drama Yeats had himself been making, if less stridently, throughout his career. His wish to restrict his audience to fifty or one hundred readers of the old epics and Yeats's plays about them echoes "Certain Noble Plays of Japan" in its claim that *At the Hawk's Well* can be performed "in a room for so little money that forty or fifty readers of poetry can pay the price" and an essay written way back in 1899, "The Theatre," where, Yeats insists, "We must make a theatre for ourselves and our friends, and for a few simple people who understand from sheer simplicity what we understand from scholarship and thought. We have planned the Irish Literary Theatre with this hospitable emotion, and that the right people may find out about us, we hope to act a play or two in the spring of every year; and that the right people may escape the stultifying memory of the theatre of commerce which clings even to them, our plays will be for the most part remote, spiritual, and ideal."[4] Then too Yeats had sought a vehicle for excluding the sciolists; then too he had sought a mode

[1] *On the Boiler* (Dublin: The Cuala Press, 1938), p. 37. Albright, commenting on this passage in *The Myth Against Myth* (London: Oxford University Press, 1972), pp. 128–29, labels it "perhaps the best gloss Yeats ever wrote on one of his poems."

[2] A major theme in his Introduction to *Fighting the Waves*, *Variorum Plays*, pp. 568–71.

[3] *Yeats's VISION and the Later Plays*, p. 237.

[4] *Essays and Introductions*, p. 166.

free of the uninspired realism pictured for the Old Man in the chambermaid face of Degas' dancers.

In the Old Man Yeats, the sedentary soul raising into being the loveliness hidden in the deeps of the mind, and Yeats, the theater manager bringing the sedentary soul's vision of loveliness to life before an audience, fuse. Self and anti-self become one. That the Old Man attacks this earliest of Yeatsian dramatic nemeses, the dreary realism of Ibsen's imitators, with near hysterical anger reflects the loss of control afflicting him and the rest of civilization as things fall apart. He is acutely aware, as Yeats was, of standing at the end of a tradition. In having the Old Man demand an audience knowing the epics and his own plays about them Yeats proclaims himself the virtual embodiment of that tradition. The Old Man is in effect his prophet, chosen—as he says, "selected" (d)—for the lonely task of carrying the truth of this tradition to an indifferent world. That the force of its truth is dying—as the Old Man is dying, as Cuchulain is dying, as Yeats knew himself to be dying—is manifest in his rejection of a mass audience because bourgeois, corrupt, and in his portrayal of the artist as outcast (his persona explaining that he had found his musicians "here and there about the streets" [ee–ff] or labelling Homer a "beggar-man"[gg]).

Bereft of values, moral or aesthetic, beyond those spun by his playwright or himself, the Old Man turns inward. He becomes a paradigm of Yeatsian subjectivity, progressively denying the world outside his own being; forgetting the name even of his father and mother; viewing art as an exclusive vocation, almost a mystery, with no roots in ordinary human experience, its success measured by its transcendence of time and materiality. He rejects carved simulations of the heads cut from Cuchulain's enemies, and with which Emer is to dance her rage and grief, because "if a dancer can dance properly no wood-carving can look as well as a parallelogram of painted wood" (ll–nn). He deprecates Degas' figures because, though "They might have looked timeless, Rameses the Great," they wear the face of "that old maid history" (vv–xx).

His speech defines both the state of crisis to which that old maid has brought a civilization verging on collapse and the

plight of the discerning individual helpless to escape civilization's collapse. He casts himself as a son of Talma because he bespeaks not only innovation in the theater but also, like Talma himself amid the ruin of the French Revolution, the integrity of the arts before an upheaval threatening to bring all to wrack. Through the Old Man, Yeats enables us to grasp the meaning of Cuchulain's death.

Directed at the present, the world of the audience rather than the past, the mythic Ireland of the *Táin Bó Cailnge*, the prologue informs the play with a complex double perspective. Much as in *Calvary*, where Christ is not living the Crucifixion but dreaming it, where he exists simultaneously as the objective consciousness doing his Father's will and the subjective consciousness who, having evolved (or revolved) through the twenty centuries of the Christian era, has become increasingly self-absorbed, *The Death of Cuchulain* focuses on the demise of ancient Celticism, imaged in the fall of its heroic ideal, while— also simultaneously—reconstructing Yeats's own dreaming back of his dramatization of the Cuchulain saga. The play is a staged reverie, a dramatic version of a mode, recurrently occupying Yeats in old age, which Albright labels the "summing-up poem"—in this sense like the poem Yeats had finished scant months before it, "The Circus Animals' Desertion."[5] The question his persona confronts in "The Circus Animals' Desertion," "What can I but enumerate old themes?" (9), he is posing in *The Death of Cuchulain* as well. He can only enumerate old themes because in a world on the edge of chaos nothing new is possible.

And in a world whose inhabitants are largely self-absorbed poetic communication is almost equally impossible—which is what the Old Man acknowledges in demanding a dance, "because where there are no words there is less to spoil" (hh–ii). To make dance rather than speech his primary dramatic vehicle is

[5] *The Myth Against Myth*, p. 59. Vendler, *Yeats's VISION*, p. 246, also notes the parallel between *The Death of Cuchulain* and "The Circus Animal's Desertion," stressing the identity of Yeats and Cuchulain, arguing that what she calls the defections of Eithne Inguba, Aoife, Maeve, even the Morrigu are comparable to the desertion of the poet by his circus animals.

to move the drama itself from a world of self-absorbed creatures, beset by time, toward the timeless world of the *Sidhe*. In
The King of the Great Clock Tower the Second Attendant
punctuates the rising of the curtain by announcing, "They
dance all day that dance in Tir-nan-oge." Whereupon the First
Attendant picks up his theme, elaborating on the nature of that
realm in which dance replaces language:

> There every lover is a happy rogue;
> And should he speak, it is the speech of birds.
> No thought has he, and therefore has no words,
> No thought because no clock, no clock because
> If I consider deeply, lad and lass,
> Nerve touching nerve upon that happy ground,
> Are bobbins where all time is wound and bound.
>
> (2–8)

The King of the Great Clock Tower too comprises somewhat
of a summing-up poem brought to the stage, the Attendants'
opening song taking its imagery from "Byzantium" and, like
"The Circus Animals' Desertion," *The Wanderings of Oisin*:
"there the hound that Oisin saw pursues/ The hornless deer
that runs in such a fright;/ And there the woman clasps an apple
tight/ For all the clamour of a famished man" (10–13). While
these works, encompassing Yeats's career from beginning to
end, all concern art's struggle against time, those of his last decade seem more and more uneasy about the adequacy of his own
art to sustain the challenge. What passes for speech in Tir-
nan-oge is wordless, spontaneous, natural, birdlike, which is to
say akin to dance. It epitomizes a total harmony, the existence
of communal assumptions of meaning on which the poet in an
increasingly fragmenting world can no longer count.

In *The Death of Cuchulain* Yeats dramatizes this view of the
inexorable decline of the West partly by repeating from *The
Only Jealousy of Emer* the liberties he has allowed himself with
his mythic model. Cuchulain is again, despite the archetype in
the tale as traditionally wrought, old—like the Old Man, like
Yeats himself. He fears that Eithne Inguba has betrayed him
because she wants a younger lover. He finds that Aoife, whom

he had challenged in *At the Hawk's Well*, and then left to bear
the son he kills in *On Baile's Strand*, has grown gray hair.

So Cuchulain, the Old Man, the cultures to which they belong, together make a constellation of images epitomizing the
power of time over all things. Yeats's hero and the producer of
his play are, like their poet, anachronisms.[6] The Old Man appears to the audience, *"looking,"* the stage directions specify,
"like something out of mythology." As he concedes of himself,
he has been chosen to produce *The Death of Cuchulain* "because I am out of fashion and out of date like the antiquated
romantic stuff the thing is made of" (d–f). And the scenario is
shaped to suggest that Cuchulain too is, even as a subject for
drama, out of date.

The play is thus without action in the conventional sense.
Like *The King's Threshold*, in which the dying Seanchan must
resist a series of temptations, each embodied in a figure of consequence in his world, to uphold the right of poets; or *Calvary*,
in which the condemned Christ must confront his failures with
Lazarus, with Judas, with the Roman soldiers, its form is pro-
cessional. In a kind of dramatic elegy to his heroic past the
doomed Cuchulain must face Eithne Inguba, Aoife, and the
Blind Man of *On Baile's Strand*, each recalling to him a crucial
episode from his adventurous life.

The first of these encounters is with Eithne Inguba, who appears announcing a heroic summons: "No matter what's the
odds, no matter though/ Your death may come of it, ride out
and fight./ The scene is set and you must out and fight" (7–9).
Cuchulain responds heroically, even to having anticipated the
call: "You have told me nothing. I am already armed" (10). But
as Eithne unwittingly implies, the heroic opportunity is an illusion: a scene, set by other hands, existing as a reality alone for
Cuchulain and his playwright—staged like the play itself. For
the end is fated, determined not only by the Morrigu but also
by the tradition behind Yeats's plot. It too is "out of mythology."

Yeats is not inventing so much as transforming, refashioning
a myth, the outlines of which have been long set by his

[6] Vendler, *Yeats's VISION*, p. 240, calls Cuchulain an anachronism.

forebears, into a symbolic projection of his mind ordering the cycles of history. Dramatically, indeed, Eithne's summons is revealed to be a subterfuge. The letter she brings from Emer bids Cuchulain not to attack but to wait. Emer's advice crystallizes his dilemma: to act prudently is to obscure himself and his few among the great host coming with Conall Cearnach on the morrow; to act heroically—which is to say according to his nature—is to commit suicide, to "face odds no man can face and live" (20). Yeats insists at the close of his dramatic career, as he had at its opening in plays like *The King's Threshold* and *On Baile's Strand*, that heroic conduct is diametrically opposed to practical wisdom. Cuchulain is out of phase with his world.

His world denies efficacy to heroic conduct; and in so doing it denies realization to the poet's dream. It denies realization to the poet's dream, of which Cuchulain's lifelong quest for self-fulfillment is an instance, because it has reached the point where that loveliness, raised into being by the toils of sedentary souls, has become impossible. It has reached the point embodied by the Hunchback in *A Vision* or the deformed Bricriu in *The Only Jealousy of Emer*.[7] Maeve has lapsed from the girl with whom Cuchulain slept, "as pretty as a bird" (39), into a monstrosity, "an eye in the middle of her forehead" (40). Cuchulain himself, recognizing that time has treated him only somewhat less unkindly, chooses to go out and die, to resume his bird shape—"My soul's first shape, a soft feathery shape" (179)—because he sees that for him such a world holds no promise.

Though his decision to seek death appears itself heroic, Yeats reduces Cuchulain's stature both through the hero's own conviction that Eithne needs a younger, friendlier man and Eithne's that the Cuchulain who has forgiven her betrayal cannot be the man she loved: "That violent man forgave no treachery" (60). The play's dynamics, moreover, undercut the very freedom to choose on which Cuchulain's claim to heroism must be based, introducing the Morrigu to stand between him and his mistress when his choice is made, implying that his determina-

[7] Vendler, *ibid.*, p. 223, makes this association between Bricriu and the Hunchback.

tion to brave the odds has been predestined by a force beyond himself.[8]

Despite his mockery of Eithne attributing her conduct to bewitchment, then warning of the Morrigu's presence—"A woman that has an eye in the middle of her forehead!/ A woman that is headed like a crow!/ But she that put those words into your mouth/ Had nothing monstrous; you put them there yourself" (41–44)—Cuchulain seems dimly aware of his plight. "I and my handful," he assures her, asserting the firmness of his heroic resolve, "are set upon the fight" (20). Yet his use of Eithne's word "set" suggests also an acknowledgment glimmering at the edges of his consciousness that the will directing this resolve may not be his own.

What saves Cuchulain from the abasement of impotence—preserves his heroic identity—is his refusal to accept impotence as his lot. When he recounts Eithne's confession of betrayal to his servant, and the servant asks if her confession is true, Cuchulain replies by declaring himself god-(or poet-)like: "I make the truth!/ I say she brings a message from my wife" (84–85). And so she does, but not the message on which he de-

---

[8] Phillip L. Marcus, "Myth and Meaning in Yeats's *The Death of Cuchulain*," *Irish University Review*, 2 (1972), 133–48, argues that the Morrrigu's entrance, after Cuchulain has chosen to ignore the letter, suggests her desire not to implement but to alter his decision, that she retains her original function as, in W.M. Hennessy's phrase, "apparently, his tutelary goddess." Marcus draws evidence for this reading not only from the play's probable sources, in Hennessy's "The Ancient Irish Goddess of War," *Revue Celtique*, I (1870–72) and in Lady Gregory's *Cuchulain of Muirthemne*, but also from Yeats's manuscript to document his case. In the manuscript, he observes, Yeats has Eithne realize that "Queen Maeve sent her foul witch [Badb]/ That has an eye in the middle of her forhead [*sic*]/ That witch has [ts. "had"] put her words into my mouth," and concludes that Yeats decided in revising to eliminate Badb as superfluous and obscure.

Whatever the manuscript or its narrative antecedents may indicate, though, their versions of the story are not what the audience sees and hears on stage. While Eithne's understanding, brought about by the Morrigu's touch, attributes to Maeve rather than the Morrigu the plot to kill Cuchulain, it is hard to conceive how the audience can discern in her anything but a foreshadowing of the hero's death, the embodiment of a force in history lying beyond his control and winding his age down to his inevitable meeting with the perpetrators of his six mortal wounds.

cides to act. In a dramatic sense his claim rests on blindness to
the reality of a world in which truth is made for him, a blindness manifest in his failure to recognize, or apparently to believe in, the monstrosity of Maeve or the existence of the Morrigu.

In another sense, however, Cuchulain is right. Comparing
Eithne's call to arms with the letter he discovers in her hand, he
observes that the letter "tells a different story" (18), then adding, "but I much prefer/ Your own unwritten words" (27–28).
Preferring Eithne's unwritten words, he acts as if she had re-
ported Emer's message faithfully, insuring that she is treated as
if she had remained loyal. As in the earlier plays of the cycle,
the hero conceives of himself as both protagonist in and shaper
of a tale. Faced with alternative directions to the narrative, different stories, he chooses the one consistent with his heroic personality. His choice becomes the substance of the drama.
Cuchulain plays out what Yeats had always averred the role of
the hero to be, making his own myth. For it is by making his
own myth that man transcends mortality. Like the artist, the
hero is subjective, self-absorbed—to use the vocabulary of *A
Vision*, an antithetical being poised, in Cuchulain's day as in
ours, on the brink of a primary age.

His antithetical nature should prove his salvation. The personal tragedy behind *The Death of Cuchulain* lies in its suggestion that Yeats, at the close of his long, productive life, no
longer believed the world would permit him even that comfort.
His doubts begin to unfold with the entrance of Aoife.

That the meeting of Cuchulain and Aoife is meant to be
viewed as scene two of the play Yeats stresses by reverting to a
Shakespearean device, signaling the end of the prior scene, the
encounter of Cuchulain and Eithne, through a shift in Eithne's
final speech from the blank verse informing the rest of their
dialogue to couplets:

> I might have peace that know
> The Morrigu, the woman like a crow,
> Stands to my defense and cannot lie,
> But that Cuchulain is about to die.
>
> (90–93)

This speech dovetails into its realization as a stage image, Cuchulain strapping himself to a pillar, dying indeed. The battle itself Yeats omits, consigning it to a momentary blackout accompanied by pipe and drum, his way of delineating the time required for Cuchulain to march out, fight his last fight, suffer his six mortal wounds, and return. He omits the battle, however, not because he could find no effective mode for presenting it—he had in fact found such a mode in the dance pantomimes of *Fighting the Waves* and *The Herne's Egg*—but because, depicting a world in which heroic action was fast becoming impossible, he excludes heroic action from his scenario.

The force undermining the potential for heroic action is embodied in Aoife: she confronts Cuchulain with stark evidence of the debility caused by the passage of years. Yeats's treatment of Aoife recalls his treatment of Maud as Ledaean body in "Among School Children," where his persona, gazing on the children, and reminded of Maud's youthful beauty, is suddenly beset by a vision of her grown old. The two images—one suggested by the fresh loveliness of the girls, the other modeled after the gaunt figures of the Quattrocentists—are abruptly juxtaposed in the speaker's mind's eye, with none of the gradualness inherent in the onset of age to soften the contrast.

Cuchulain recognizing Aoife experiences the same shock. The Aoife he remembers is the beautiful queen with whom he had fought and slept; the Aoife before him is old, her beauty decayed. What the dialogue Yeats gives them stresses is the erosive power of time, which has brought this change about:

> *Aoife*. Am I recognised, Cuchulain?
> *Cuchulain*.   You fought with a sword,
>   It seemed that we should kill each other, then
>   Your body wearied and I took your sword.
> *Aoife*. But look again, Cuchulain! Look again!
> *Cuchulain*. Your hair is white.
> *Aoife*.   That time was long ago,
>   And now it is my time. I have come to kill you.
>   (94–99)

Age has destroyed not only Aoife's beauty but also her courage. She fears Cuchulain, as she had not when he challenged her with a sword, and, though he is weak with wounds, binds his hands with her veil. Aoife winding her veil about the stone and fastening Cuchulain's hands to it repeats the movement of the grey of Macha making his protective circle around his master and recalls, if remotely, Hades' bobbin in "Byzantium" "bound in mummy-cloth." Yeats behind Aoife is declaring to his audience that Cuchulain is being mumified, preserved, by the play and the cycle to which it belongs. The meeting of Cuchulain and Aoife thus unfolds against memories of the heroic past dramatized in *At the Hawk's Well* and *On Baile's Strand*, and evoked through the exchange between them:

> *Aoife.*   I was afraid,
> But now that I have wound you in the veil
> I am not afraid. But—how did my son fight?
> *Cuchulain.* Age makes more skilful but not better men.
> *Aoife.* I have been told you did not know his name
> And wanted, because he had a look of me,
> To be his friend, but Conchubar forbade it.
> *Cuchulain.* Forbade it and commanded me to fight;
> That very day I had sworn to do his will,
> Yet refused him, and spoke about a look;
> But somebody spoke of witchcraft and I said
> Witchcraft had made the look, and fought and killed him.
> Then I went mad, I fought against the sea.
> *Aoife.* I seemed invulnerable; you took my sword,
> You threw me on the ground and left me there.
> I searched the mountain for your sleeping-place
> And laid my virgin body at your side,
> And yet, because you had left me, hated you,
> And thought that I would kill you in your sleep
> And yet begot a son that night between
> Two black thorn-trees.

>   (126–46)

As in *On Baile's Strand*, Cuchulain's fight with the sea becomes a paradigm of Ireland's decline from her heroic age. Having killed his son, he is without issue. He has irrevocably sub-mitted himself to the will of Conchubar, Yeats's embodiment of the pragmatic sanction. The hero's sole escape from his abase-ment lies in madness and death—challenging the waves.

The heroic nature of this recalled scene lies in the purity of the passions engendering it: hate and love carried to their logi-cal extremes, war to the death and sexual congress. As Cuchul-ain had long before insisted, in defending his fondness for a woman dedicated to his ruin and the ruin of the land he serves, "no wonder at all in that./ I have never known love but as a kiss/ In the mid-battle, and a difficult truce/ Of oil and water" (*OBS*, 331–34). But such clean, simple, unambiguous responses, based on shared values which make possible a kiss in mid-battle, have disappeared before the growing corruption of the world. What has replaced them is epitomized by the Blind Man, the last of the images called up from Cuchulain's past.

The return, at the climax to *The Death of Cuchulain*, of the figure who had served as comic surrogate for Conchubar in *On Baile's Strand* suggests a world so fallen from the ideal Cuchulain enacts that potential for action rests alone with his antithesis. The Blind Man labels himself "A blind old beggar-man" (153); and his assumption of this role, echoing the characterization of Homer as "beggar-man" by the play's em-bittered producer, is emphasized through an incremental repeti-tion in the dialogue, underscoring the word "beggar":

> Cuchulain.　　　　　　　I think you are a blind old man.
> Blind Man. A blind old beggar-man.
>
> 　　　　　　　　　　　　　　　　　(152–53)

That the Blind Man cuts a figure (at least rhetorically) akin to Homer's indicates how slim are the chances of poetry in this world. For he has anything but a poetic soul.

He is, in fact, the arch-materialist, having agreed to kill Cuchulain for twelve pennies.[9] His murder forms, as Yeats's title suggests, the central symbolic moment of the play, crystal-lizing the demise of the heroic ideal at the hands of the prag-

[9] In this reading of the Blind Man's role I am largely anticipated by Donald R. Pearce, "Yeats's Last Plays: An Interpretation," *ELH*, xviii (1951), 76.

matic sanction. When Cuchulain remarks ironically, "Twelve pennies! What better reason for killing a man?" (170), we are reminded that he too has killed men, but in the scheme of values governing his civilization for truly good and sufficient reasons. When the Blind Man justifies himself by boasting his "good sense" (175), we are reminded that Cuchulain shows bad sense—by seeking the Well of Immortality, gazing into its Guardian's unmoistened eyes, and striking out after Aoife; by laying his head on the Red Man's block; by fighting the waves; by marching off to battle against Emer's advice. But he shows nobility. Good sense is alone a virtue among the decadent types, the Conchubars of the world, who have arisen to subdue its Cuchulains. In *On Baile's Strand* and *At the Hawk's Well* it is the fool and the idiot who are capable of the abandon required to act heroically.

The Blind Man's blindness, then, is ultimately moral blindness, reflecting not only his failure but also the failure of the order he embodies. Cuchulain turns from him, as he turns from that order, to contemplate the soft feathery shape his soul will acquire at death, to announce that "it is about to sing" (183). Death transforms the hero into his anti-self: the warrior become artist, his soul singing as Homer is said to sing. "And," as Cuchulain remarks of the shape his soul is to take, "is not that a strange shape for the soul/ Of a great fighting-man?" (180–81).

The shape Cuchulain's soul takes renders him akin to the lovers in Tir-nan-oge, speaking the speech of birds, or to the Shrouds in the poem Yeats wrote immediately after his play, and which he described to Edith Shackleton Heald as a sequel to it, "Cuchulain Comforted."[10] Those Shrouds too are birdlike; and the stance Cuchulain assumes—leaning "upon a tree/ As though to meditate on wounds and blood" (5–6)—as they stare out of the branches at him parallels the stance he assumes, strapped to the stone, in the play itself. The poem, that is, partly recapitulates the conflict of the play, not in this world but in a

[10] Wade, *Letters*, p. 922. Wilson, *W.B. Yeats and Tradition* (New York: Macmillan, 1958), p. 244, cites this letter as evidence for his claim that any discussion of *The Death of Cuchulain* must take "Cuchulain Comforted" into account.

Purgatory implied by the *terza rima* stanzas and the wooded setting (both elements suggestive of Dante) in which its narrative unfolds. Cuchulain must, as the seeming authority of the place urges, give over meditating on wounds and blood to "Obey our ancient rule and make a shroud" (13).

To make a shroud is to become one. The dead are their shrouds; which is to say that Cuchulain is being invited to refashion himself. And the new self to emerge from this refashioning will be his opposite. The shrouds he is being asked to join are "Convicted cowards all" (21). They are, however, singers too, again like the lovers in Tir-nan-oge or like the shape Cuchulain foresees his soul taking after death:

> They sang, but had nor human tunes nor words,
> Though all was done in common as before;
> They had changed their throats and had the throats of birds.
> (23–25)

Yeats would have us perceive in death, then, a kind of creativity—in the world of the play (our world) perhaps the one kind of creativity still possible. As in *The King's Threshold* and *Deirdre*, the hero by dying rises into myth. From the ruins of time he builds a mansion in eternity.

In *The Death of Cuchulain* the building of this mansion has special poignancy. For it emerges against the backdrop of Yeats's own impending death. The play seems almost a dramatization of Yeats, projected into Cuchulain, his heroic mask, confronting the darkness before him and exploring the potential for an immortality beyond. In *Swan and Shadow* Whitaker perceptively characterizes Yeats's dramatic method by quoting R. G. Collingwood on his approach to writing history: "I plunge beneath the surface of my mind and there live a life in which I not merely think about Nelson but am Nelson, and thus in thinking about Nelson think about myself. . . ."[11] Yeats thinking about Cuchulain is Yeats thinking about himself. As the play proper consists of the poet extending his consciousness into the figure of the warrior, its epilogue consists of

[11] *Swan and Shadow*, p. 204.

the warrior extending his consciousness into a fictive surrogate for the poet.

Yeats underscores this shifting focus through his manipulation of the scenario's final sequence: setting it partly in the world of the supernatural, giving it to the Morrigu; then returning it to the world of Cuchulain, in Emer's dance; and bringing down the curtain on a scene from the modern world, in the Street-Singer's performance at *"some Irish Fair of our day."* The Morrigu evokes the realm in which all heroes, alien to an abased present (Emer's, our own), have come to reside. She arranges the dance accompanied by the notes of a bird, Cuchulain's soul having begun to sing. Yet she, no more than Cuchulain, no more than Yeats himself, can control the course of history.

So the dance yields to the music of that contemporary Irish Fair, and to the lament of the harlot sung by the Street-Singer. The play reverts to the decadent culture the Old Man has reviled in his prologue. Mythic imagination, the Street-Singer's song suggests, survives only in the outcast, the prostitute, who alone meets "Conall, Cuchulain, Usna's boys,/ All that most ancient race" (198–99). Making her the repository of myth is comparable to making Homer a beggar-man, or to putting the affirmation of the reality behind myth into the mouth of a singer singing about a singer singing to a beggar-man. It stresses the extent of the world's lapse from its heroic age, measures how far modern man is removed from his heroic forebears.

That the singer in the song is a harlot emphasizes the sensual quality to her apprehension of life, and so the unbridgeable gap between her and the ideal encompassed by Conall, Cuchulain, Usna's boys. Maeve may have had "three in an hour," but the harlot "can get/ No grip upon their thighs" (200 and 202–203). Caught between her adoration of "those clever eyes/ Those muscular bodies" (201–202) and her powerlessness to experience them physically, she poses what is, for Yeats as for her, the overwhelming question: "Are those things that men adore and loathe/ Their sole reality?" (212–13). Things men adore and loathe are things capable of material possession—for the harlot, the "still some living/ That do my limbs unclothe"

(208–209). Her refusal to acknowledge them—the material world—her sole reality is implied by the sudden shift of her attention from her lovers to Ireland's nearest imitators of that most ancient race, the martyrs of Easter Week: "What stood in the Post Office/ With Pearse and Connolly?/ What comes out of the mountain/ Where men first shed their blood?/ Who thought Cuchulain till it seemed/ He stood where they had stood?" (214–19). Pearse and Connolly calling up their heroic natures undergo the same process as Collingwood thinking himself into Nelson or Yeats thinking himself into Cuchulain. The Cuchulain with whom they fuse themselves arises from their imaginations.

But, Yeats is moved to ask, of what efficacy is Cuchulain? Of what efficacy are the imaginations calling him up? Though Yeats continues to insist on the artist's unique power to render the heroic spirit concrete—"A statue's there to mark the place,/ By Oliver Sheppard done" (224–25)—he has muted the faith, proclaimed in plays like *The King's Threshold*, that hanging "Images of the life what was in Eden/ About the childbed of the world" might engender "Triumphant children." No modern woman has borne a body like Cuchulain's. Art provides at most a platform from which an Old Man, Yeats or another, can look with scorn on life. Here, at the end of his magnificent career, facing a world that rejects his values and his vocation, Yeats is compelled to see his art as a tale sung by a harlot to a beggarman.

Index

Albert, Henri, 53
Albright, Daniel, 130, 131n, 134
Anima Mundi, 9, 17, 29, 30, 31, 39, 78, 92, 93, 112, 123, 124
Antheil, George, 114

Beckett, Samuel, 77, 107
Benson, Frank Robert, 93
Bernhardt, Sarah, 71, 93
Bjersby, Birgit, 68–69
Blake, William, 6, 12–13, 17, 19, 21, 27, 30, 86, 128; "Descriptive Catalogue of Pictures, A," 13; *Europe*, 27, 28; *Marriage of Heaven and Hell, The*, 27
Bloom, Harold, xiii, 33n, 40, 101–102
Blunt, Wilfrid Scawen, 70–71, 83, 120
Bornstein, George, 101
Bradford, Curtis B., 95n, 98n, 104n, 105n
Bridges, Robert, 40–42
Brown, Ford Madox, 45
Bushrui, A. B., 69n

Castiglione, Baldassare, 78–79, 82
Chaucer, Geoffrey, 13
Clark, David R., 10, 12n, 63
Coleridge, Samuel Taylor, 98, 110
Collingwood, R. G., 143, 145
Connolly, James, 145
Craig, Edward Gordon, 15n, 16–17, 18, 91–92, 93

Daimon in Yeatsian tragedy, 14
dance in drama, 16, 139
Dante Alighieri, 143
Desai, Rupin W., 3n, 6, 26
double-plot as structural device, 4, 23, 26, 29, 62–63
Dowden, Edward, 6
Dulac, Edmund, 92

Elizabethan drama, 93–94
Ellis, Edwin, 12
Ellmann, Richard, 10n, 12n, 95, 96, 106n
Emmet, Robert, 81
Engelberg, Edward, 11n, 18

Fay, Frank, 30
Fenollosa, Ernest, 18, 91
Fergusson, Francis, 10
Fitzgerald, Edward, 81
Flaubert, Gustave, 111–12

Goethe, Johann Wolfgang von, 71, 95
Gonne, Maud, 96, 100, 139
Greek drama, 3, 11, 15, 23, 58, 89–90
Gregory, Isabel Augusta, 7, 15, 44; *Cuchulain of Muirthemne*, 32, 68, 73, 82, 115, 120, 137n
Grossman, Allan R., 111

Heald, Edith Shackleton, 142
Hearne, Lafcadio, 112
Hennessy, W. W., 137n
heroic in Yeats, xiii, 46, 77–82, 103–105, 136, 138, 143
history as recurrent cycles, 21–23, 111, 130, 135–36
Holinshed, Raphael, 94
Homer, 42, 141, 142, 144
Howarth, Herbert, 81

Ibsen, Henrik, 13, 71
Ito, Michio, 8, 9, 62, 92

Keats, John: *Eve of Saint Agnes, The*, 108; "*La Belle Dame Sans Merci*," 32, 110, 116–17, 118, 122
Kermode, Frank, 109

Leeper, Janet, 16n

147

PRINCETON ESSAYS IN LITERATURE

Library of Congress Cataloging in Publication Data

Friedman, Barton R.
  Adventures in the deeps of the mind.

  (Princeton essays in literature)
  Includes bibliographical references and index.
  1. Yeats, William Butler, 1865–1939—Characters—
Cuchulain.   2. Cuchulain.   I. Title.
PR5908.C8F7   822'.8   76–45897
ISBN 0–691–06325–7

6916